build your business on ideas

A PRACTICAL GUIDE TO BUSINESS CREATIVITY

JODIE NEWMAN

This edition published in the UK
in 2019 by Icon Books Ltd,
Omnibus Business Centre,
39–41 North Road,
London N7 9DP
email: info@iconbooks.com
www.iconbooks.com

First published in the UK
in 2013 by Icon Books

Sold in the UK, Europe and Asia
by Faber & Faber Ltd,
Bloomsbury House,
74–77 Great Russell Street,
London WC1B 3DA
or their agents

Distributed in South Africa
by Jonathan Ball,
Office B4, The District,
41 Sir Lowry Road,
Woodstock 7925

Distributed in Australia and
New Zealand
by Allen & Unwin Pty Ltd,
PO Box 8500,
83 Alexander Street,
Crows Nest,
NSW 2065

Distributed in Canada
by Publishers Group Canada,
76 Stafford Street, Unit 300
Toronto,
Ontario M6J 2S1

Distributed in the USA
by Publishers Group West,
1700 Fourth Street,
Berkeley, CA 94710

ISBN: 978-178578-469-9

Typeset in Avenir by Marie Doherty

Printed and bound in Great Britain by Clays Ltd, Elcograf S.p.A.

About the Author

Jodie Newman has run her own creative and strategic business, The Business Allotment, for over fifteen years. She initially trained at the Royal College of Art as a furniture designer before entering the commercial world of marketing and procurement – it was here that she realized that innovative thinking was 'the difference that made the difference' to businesses. She is now a highly experienced business strategist, creative thinking trainer and speaker, who runs strategic and creative workshops and training for companies and individuals who want to improve their creative thinking and grow their business.

Contents

Introduction

In an increasingly competitive business world, both individuals and companies need to be able to set themselves apart from the rest while running an efficient business. As processes, transactions, manufacturing and a whole host of other operational activities become increasingly automated and efficient, what is it that will propel a business to be better than its competitors? In a word: IDEAS. Ideas are the most valuable currency of our business landscape and will only become more important in the future. Why? Because creativity cannot be automated. You may be able to buy a machine that will churn out your cupcakes faster, in any flavour that the customer desires, but it will not generate the ideas needed to make your cupcakes better, tastier, more innovative or more beautiful. Nor will it come up with new ideas for other tasty treats to help you grow your business. An automated customer telephone service might be brilliant at taking payment or giving order statuses, but it is pretty rubbish at thinking of new ways to impress and delight customers.

This book is for anyone who wants to be better at coming up with ideas, whether on an individual level or within a team, department or company. Working with businesses of all sizes for the last ten years, I have met people who say they could 'never be creative', those who purport to be 'ideas people', and plenty in between. But both labels can be misleading. If you feel you struggle to come up with ideas and be creative, this book will give you a range of easy-to-use tools that can be called on at any time. These tools can be put to use with a pencil and the back of an envelope, or a set of marker pens and a flip chart – it doesn't matter. What matters is that you approach each tool with an open mind, a belief that you *can* have good ideas and that the process of generating them will be fun ... and easy.

For business owners, this book will provide a great starting point to weave creativity into everything you do. There is some value in announcing: 'Right, we need better ideas to get ahead of our competitors, let's have a brainstorm', but far more in applying this creative intent across the whole business, making it part of your vision and strategic plan, allowing everyone to be part of the process and thus reaping far more reward as a result. We will look in detail at how to build a creative culture – everything from the physical environment to measuring your creative output.

There is no size of business that cannot embrace creativity. I have worked with start-ups who, being small and agile, often have a natural ability to create ideas, try them out, refine and perfect them. As these businesses grow, it is often my task to recapture that original creative spark and rekindle it in an organization ten times larger. This book will help businesses create a structure around encouraging and protecting ideas to ensure that this creative agility is never lost and can only flourish. For larger businesses that are realizing that creativity may well be their only competitive advantage in the coming years, there is a fantastic opportunity to create positive change and allow any employee to become part of the ideas process that will shape the business. The suggestions in this book can be made wholesale, or implemented one by one. What is important with bigger organizations is that change – and the context of change – is communicated clearly. With people who embrace the creative challenge to make a better business, ideas can quickly become the lifeblood of an organization and its success.

Whether you are an individual wanting to improve your levels of creativity, or a CEO or management team wishing to put ideas at the very heart of your business, there is one thing you must undertake if you going to succeed: practice. When I mention this word in my creative thinking training workshops, it more often than not elicits a grumble. Practice? Groan. It sounds a bit too much like homework for most people's liking. But there is no magic wand to wave that will make people or businesses more creative. It takes a little time and effort. Imagine there is a creative muscle in your brain, lying unused among the synapses. When you start to generate ideas, just as when you do exercise for the first time in a long time and use muscles that you forgot you had, it feels a bit unnatural and strange. The odd twinge is not uncommon. But the more you use the creative tools in this book, the easier it will feel. Every time you sit down – or stand in the shower – to think up ideas, that creative muscle will get stronger, and better at what it is supposed to do. Before long you will be able to summon any number of ways of looking at a problem, and your only issue will be finding a piece of paper big enough to capture them all.

I have run my business, Creative Consulting, for over ten years. What gets me out of bed each morning is my passion for putting creativity and ideas at the very core of a business and watching the difference that it makes – to the staff, to the customers and to the bottom line. I have worked with new businesses that wanted to launch their products to the world in a creative way, marketing agencies that needed killer ideas to help them win pitches, recently merged companies looking to create a 'best of both worlds' culture, retailers that sought new ideas to make them stand out from the crowded high street, media organizations that wanted to give every member of staff better ways of solving business challenges, news organizations that wanted to define their own creative future, and multinationals that wanted Europe-wide promotion ideas to win them more market share. The variety of businesses I help is endless, but the desire is common to all: they have recognized that creativity can have a huge and sustainable impact on the success of what they do.

I have used all of the tools and approaches described in this book many times, so know that they work with all manner of businesses, no matter what shape or size. Like all good tools, they can be misappropriated and used flexibly to suit your needs (I have been known to bang a nail into a wall with a pair of pliers, which did the job just fine). One of the greatest parts of my job is going back to a business with which I have previously worked, setting up a creative process and teaching a number of creative thinking tools, to see how they have made them their own. I encourage you to do the same with the techniques in this book.

This book is intended to be as practical as possible. It is not a theory of creativity, but a practical guide to making ideas work for you and your business. I will take you through the stages of the creative process so that you can see how simple coming up with an idea can be. The focus then turns to growing a culture of creativity within your business and engaging your staff in the process. The central section is the creative tool kit – a wide range of creative thinking techniques that can be applied to any challenge. And finally, I talk about the critical part of the process: evaluating and implementing your ideas. By the end of the book, you will have the means to make your business one that counts ideas among its most valuable assets.

So what is creativity, anyway?

Being creative is big news for businesses and there has been much discussion of late as to why creativity is essential for businesses. In *A Whole New Mind* by Daniel Pink, the term 'Conceptual Age' is used to describe our current stage of commerce and the critical contribution that creativity makes to modern business survival; in *Disciplined Dreaming*, Josh Linkner calls this the 'Age of Creativity'. Business thinkers and creativity experts all seem to agree:

without creativity, businesses that exist right now will fail in the future.

So what exactly is creativity, where can you get it and how can you build it into your business? This book will take you through these points step by step, and give you practical, effective tools for changing your business through creativity, from initial brainwave to final application. If you are in any doubt as to the importance of making this change, I talk later about the benefits of making ideas central to everything a business does, but I fundamentally believe that as the economy and business landscape shifts and reshapes, creative businesses – be they accountancies, manufacturers or retailers – will be the ones left standing.

Look up any definition of creativity and there will be mention of new ideas, the imagination, of bringing something into being that did not previously exist and of originality. Ken Robinson, a thought leader in innovation and creativity, calls it 'the process of having original ideas that have value'. It is these original ideas that will help your business stand out from the crowd and win more customers, and it is that value that will be added to your bottom line. The value can be financial: just look at Apple. In his 2006 article 'How the iPod changed Apple's fortunes', Jim Dalrymple explores how the ideas that led to the iPod transformed Apple. Interestingly, the device was not the first mp3 player on the market: it was not a breakthrough idea that brought financial success for Apple the first time. Rather, it was a combination of innovations in interface, software and service that created the difference. The value that ideas can bring will often reach out beyond just the financial benefit. Ideas can enhance your reputation and your brand, which in itself adds value back into the business. And ideas that bring your customers a better experience create valuable customer loyalty – do your products or services engender the same level of loyalty that an Apple product does?

The world, and particularly the business world, can sometimes appear to be divided into two camps: the creative people, and the non-creative people; the pushing-the-boundaries people, and the building-the-boundaries people – and people often have preconceived ideas about who fits into which category. Which do you consider yourself?

There is a great, classic creativity test (the Torrance Test of Creative Thinking, developed by Dr J.P. Torrance), which tests one particular and essential component of creativity: divergent thinking.

Divergent thinking

Divergent thinking is one of the key facets of the creative process. It is the process whereby you generate as many different options, ideas and interpretations about a single topic or challenge as you possibly can. The purpose of divergent thinking is to enable you to see different aspects of a situation, which in turn helps you to create original ideas.

TRY IT NOW!

Grab a paper clip, a house brick, a spoon, a bottle of water or any other everyday object you have to hand – and make sure you have a pen and paper. Give yourself one minute to write down as many uses as you can think of for your item. Now count how many different thoughts or ideas you generated in 60 seconds. How did you do?

On average, an adult will manage perhaps ten. For example, for a paper clip their list might include ideas such as: clip to hold papers together, hair clip, cufflinks or bookmark. Highly creative people who are practised in divergent thinking might score up to 200, and their list may contain ideas such as an obstacle in a flea circus, a clamp to keep two drinking straws together or a tool for cleaning under your fingernails. You can also analyse the ideas by looking at four different criteria, or sub-categories of divergent thinking:

Fluency – this is the abundance of your 'flow' of ideas, measured by how many ideas you generate within the time; the most common way to measure divergent thinking in a test such as this.

Originality – this is how original (or uncommon) the ideas are. The flea circus idea is more original than, say, a bookmark, so would score more highly here.

Flexibility – this is how flexible you are in your creative thinking, measured by how many different areas or topics your list covers. Hair clip and cufflinks, for example, are within the same area (dress), but the flea circus, drinking straw clamp and fingernail cleaner are all ideas from different areas.

Elaboration – this is how detailed your ideas are. 'Bookmark', as an idea, is about as simple as a paper clip idea can get, while a clamp to hold two drinking straws together is a more elaborate use of the paperclip and would score more highly.

If your score was closer to the lower end of the scale, do not worry – the key word here is 'practised'. In 2009 the *Harvard Business Review* published 'The Innovator's DNA', the culmination of six years' study of business executives and entrepreneurs. The report concluded that creative capacity was only 20 per cent 'inherent' within individuals – and that therefore 80 per cent of creative ability was learned. The tools and techniques in this book will help you to develop and exercise your divergent thinking muscles and creative skills as part of a tool kit designed to weave creativity into everything you do.

Why do businesses need to think and act differently?

In most industries, the marketplace is crowded. Think of a recent product or service that you purchased and how many alternatives you had to choose from. For me, a recent online shopping trip for a kettle saw me choosing from over 50 options – and all I wanted to do was make a cup of tea. Rarely does a brand new market appear containing only a single business, which can enjoy the solitude of being able to sell its exclusive product or service without competition. And even then the business in that fortunate position will soon be facing stiff opposition from other companies creating their own versions and jostling for market share. What do these businesses, and those that enter an already crowded market, need more than anything else? A competitive edge. And how do they get that? With great ideas.

Consumers have huge choice when it comes to the products and services they need; in most instances now, they can choose via the internet a vast range of products and services from a global marketplace. So using creativity to stand out – whether this be to develop new products, a new way of providing a service, or a new way to sell – is absolutely essential. And it is not just about making small, incremental improvements; it can be about looking for new ways to do what you do that will radically transform the product, service or marketplace.

> *The best way to create value is to innovate*
> *your way ahead of the competition.*
> Paul Sloane, *The Leader's Guide to Lateral Thinking Skills*

Products and services are either a commodity, or have added value. For example, if you manufacture bread, you may well be selling it at a commodity level; having to price it at market rate, or under, in order to compete with the myriad of other bread manufacturers who are also offering basic white, brown and granary sliced loaves. This is arguably the toughest business environment to be in, as you have the most competition for the least return. However, if you apply the creative process to your product range and spend time generating ideas to evolve the product – or indeed, create a breakthrough product that redefines the 'bread' category – then your products are no longer just commodities.

In 2010 Marks & Spencer Bakery wanted to boost bakery sales with new ideas to build incremental sales. They embarked on a creative process which involved gaining fresh customer insights and generating ideas, and produced the innovative Half & Half Super Soft Loaf, which contained sliced white bread on one side and wholemeal bread on the other – thus ending the age-old struggle for parents who were being badgered into buying white bread for their kids while preferring brown for themselves. The product was accompanied by another innovation: the packaging opened and could be resealed at both ends. It was one of the most successful lines that M&S launched in their bakery department that year. And what was the one significant thing that facilitated the improvement? The application of creativity.

There is a second, equally compelling reason why your business should put creativity at the top of the agenda: brain capital.

Brain capital
Brain capital is the sum of the all the brains that work in an organization. Every person that applies their brain to a problem can generate ideas, particularly if given encouragement and the appropriate tools. Creativity thrives when a diverse mix of brains from different parts of the organization come together to generate ideas – often the best ideas come from someone who can approach the problem from a totally new perspective. How well are you using your brain capital?

Each brain in your business has the potential to bring fresh, creative ideas to bear on what they do – and yet it is amazing how many businesses fail to exploit this capital. Does your company have processes or activities in place that make the most of your brain capital? If not, this book will show you how to put these in place. It is incredibly important to recognize that everyone can contribute – and encouraging everyone to have a voice is not just a sound commercial decision, but means that staff will be happier and feel more involved in the business: an ideal atmosphere for further creativity.

CASE STUDY

A few years ago, I worked with a marketing agency to help them get their creative mojo back – they complained that their pitch concepts were often very similar to each other, and that there was no real originality in the campaign ideas that they were coming up with. This was a real problem as they lived or died by their ability to wow the potential client with fresh new ideas that would mark them out as a creative, credible and income-generating marketing partner.

I started by talking to the senior team about what they wanted their agency to be famous for, and they were all crystal clear: they wanted to be famous for great ideas. This would attract both the best brands to work with the agency and the best talent to work within it. So why, when the wish was there at the top of the business, was it not happening?

I spent some time there, talking to the client services teams and creative teams, as well as the other internal departments, and attended a couple of their brainstorms. The cause of the problem became clear immediately: these sessions were attended by the same few 'ideas people' every time, with the same person in control of the flip chart. There was no brief, but simply a quick, verbal outline of the problem. The meeting room was populated by people from the same client team, and there were no representatives from the creative department, let alone reception, accounts or HR. One of the senior team held court at the flip chart, writing down only those ideas that they felt 'made the grade'. I watched as certain people in the room realized that their ideas were not making it to the board and eventually stopped contributing. The session was controlled by the senior person and a handful of others who were obviously considered the 'ideas people', who dominated the session and tended to dismiss, subconsciously or otherwise, ideas that came from other people. At one point, the senior person started to write up his own ideas without sharing them with the group at all. Toward the end of the 'brainstorm', he chose the strongest idea that they would then develop, which just so happened to be one of his own ideas from the beginning of the session. All in all, it was about the least fun and productive creative discussion I have ever seen.

It was no surprise that their thinking was stuck in a rut. No matter how creative a person is, there will be patterns to their creative process. They will subconsciously use the same range of tools to create new ideas, and when this is reinforced by working on similar client briefs with the same group of people – who also have the same type of creative thoughts as they always have – the thinking will quickly go stale.

There were two ways in which this issue could be tackled: from a business culture perspective and as a process change in terms of how they generated their ideas. We started with the latter, as this is often the quickest way to demonstrate the value of a new way of being creative. As the key issue for their brainstorms was that they were leaving the majority of their brain capital out of the process, we started there. For every idea generation session that the agency held from then on, the rule was to include representatives from across the business. Bringing brain capital together in this way produced a myriad of fresh perspectives on the challenges they were facing, and this brought new ideas from all corners of the organization that would have otherwise not been heard. Along with this new way of using their brain capital, I introduced a more structured way of running the idea generation session to allow everyone to fully contribute, and trained them to use new creative tools that would break old thinking habits and force new ideas to the fore.

There was inevitably resistance from the creative department, who felt that a new way of 'doing ideas' was encroaching on their territory of expertise. They were the ideas people, after all, and so didn't need help with coming up with them. I could have talked to them until there was no oxygen left in the room, trying to convince them that their creative talent could benefit from using new tools and that these tools would help reinvigorate their thinking. I could have preached all day that working with other parts of the business rather than being cloistered away from everyone else would be of huge creative benefit. But instead, I simply invited them all to an ideas session and tackled a current brief. As their brains – alongside those of their colleagues from reception, finance and production – were taken along unfamiliar creative thinking paths, and new insights were being generated, a few of them even uncrossed their arms. By the end of the session, and well over 150 ideas later, it was clear to them that the process had something to offer everyone.

As these new ideas sessions went on, and proved to be a success in terms of converting pitches to business wins, I then went back into the business to train a handful of employees to facilitate the sessions themselves, so that they could really get the most out of the brain capital in the room. The next time I returned to the agency was to run a large ideas session that included the prospective client team who had given them a pitch brief: now that really was making the most of their brain capital.

Despite the notion of creativity in a business context sometimes conjuring ideas of a structure-less, directionless chaos – anathema to the quiet control many organizations are aiming for – this is far from the truth. There is nothing to fear from letting creativity rule your organization, and with the processes and tools explained in this book, you can transform your team, your department or your business into one where creativity is at the heart of everything you do, and so begin to reap the financial and cultural rewards. The only side effects could be increased motivation, high morale and a growing sense of job satisfaction among your staff.

1. The Creative Process

In order to think creatively, it's important to first understand how ideas are formed. The romantic version of the creative process often involves a lone, tortured artist trapped in painful penance in an unfurnished hut as he pours his angst onto canvas, or an eccentric inventor with unruly hair tinkering in his shed trying to perfect his time machine. Luckily, the creative process that many creative theorists talk about, and that which forms the bedrock of the idea generation system that I use, is considerably easier to adopt. There are four key stages:

- Preparation
- Incubation
- Illumination
- Evaluation.

This model of creativity was first posited by the social psychologist Graham Wallas in 1926 and has formed the basis of many theories of creativity since. Whether you are an individual or an organization engaged in creating new ideas, it is important to understand these steps so that you can give time to the process and have a system in place that reflects these key stages of creativity to encourage ideas. If you keep these four key stages in mind when you begin the work of generating ideas, whether individually or in a group, you will work with the natural process that the brain undertakes when being creative.

People who are well versed in generating ideas – in being creative – often go through these stages quite subconsciously. The brain is like a muscle: asking it to do something new can feel, strange, unnatural and forced, but with practice it gets easier. However, while the process may sound like a cumbersome and long-winded way to get to a new idea, these four stages represent something that can happen in your brain in a matter of seconds. For example, say you are walking to the shops to buy dinner, as you have a friend joining you tonight whom you haven't seen for a while. 'What shall I get for dinner?' you muse. You walk some more, whistling as you go, and you spot a kid with a cowboy hat on. 'Oh, we could have steak … or beef wellington …' you think (once your brain has gone from cowboys to steak, probably via a cattle ranch). You then see a poster advertising a circus. 'What about pudding … custard? Maybe with apple pie?' (Your brain immediately pictured a circus clown, with a custard pie hurtling toward his face). You are nearly at the shops when you hear some-one speaking Italian, and suddenly think: 'Ah, maybe we could have pasta instead?' As you pull a trolley toward you, you weigh up the options and decide that steak is a little pricey, and beef wellington will involve too much prepar-ation when you could be catching up with your friend. So pasta it is.

And there you have it – the creative process in action:

- Preparation – wondering what to get for dinner

- Incubation – walking and letting inspiration affect your thinking

- Illumination – the ideas

- Evaluation – weighing up all the options.

This thinking process happens hundreds of times a day without you even knowing about it, and so if you consider yourself 'not an ideas person' you probably need to think again.

 Eighty per cent of your creative ability can be learned … so ideas can and should come from anyone. By following the four-stage creative process and the tools in this book, anyone in your organization can begin to make valuable contributions to your business.

Let's look at the four stages of the creative process in a little more detail. As you use these stages to structure your own creative process, it may well feel a bit awkward and cumbersome to begin with. However, like practising a tennis swing or playing the piano, the more you practise, the more easily you will do it. Eventually, the stages of creativity will simply be part of your everyday thought process, and you won't need to go through them consciously (although it can still be a useful exercise to do so).

Preparation

Preparation is essential to achieving a creative output, but can sometimes be overlooked in the rush to get to the 'ideas bit'. This is a critical mistake. It is all very well deciding to make a cake, getting out the bowl and spoon and adding ingredients as they occur to you, but if you haven't put the preparation in there is every chance that you will get some way down the line only to discover that you've got no flour, you ate the last of the jam for breakfast and you haven't got a cake tin.

So taking time to analyse the challenge that you are facing will pay dividends further down the line. This analysis creates a much deeper understanding of the challenge, which will help create richer and more original ideas.

It is also critical that during the preparation stage that you start to uncover any underlying assumptions that are latent in your understanding of the brief, which could stifle your creativity. For example, your business challenge might be to get more sales with your three-person sales force, but your staff cannot possibly fit more prospective client visits into their working day. The obvious solution to the problem is to either employ more sales people or make them work overtime. But what is the assumption here? One of them is that to create a sale, the sales person needs to visit the prospect. Remove this assumption and you can immediately see many other solutions – such as for all the prospects to come to you for a sales seminar, or for your sales people to offer Skype meetings to demonstrate that you really value your clients' time.

 Assumptions are a real creativity killer. It is often hard to recognize that you are working with assumptions, as they can be easily mistaken for cold, hard facts. Make sure you spot them so you can explore all avenues when generating ideas.

In this 'preparation' stage, there is a useful tool I often employ to help people really get under the skin of the problem and ensure that all contributing factors are uncovered: Ladder Analysis.

Ladder Analysis

This tool works equally well if you are working individually or in a group – but if the latter, make sure you work on a scale large enough to suit the group, with either a flip chart or large whiteboard.

1. Across the top of your page, write your challenge as you see it. For example: 'How to get a lot more people to visit our website and purchase online.'

2. Under this challenge, draw a ladder with just a top rung:

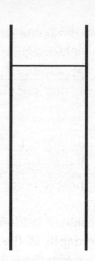

3. On this top rung, write down a key reason why you think you are not getting enough website visitors. For example, this could be because people do not know the website address.

4. Consider this reason, and ask yourself: why? Now draw in a second rung and jot down on this rung the reason why – such as the fact that you have not advertised the website address.

5. Keep asking 'why?' to the reasons that you write on each rung, extending your ladder downwards until you run out of answers.

6. Now go back to the challenge statement at the top of the page, and draw a new ladder beneath it. Consider another element that is part of the problem: in this instance, it could be that people prefer buying your product in a shop.

7. Work your way down the ladder in the same way as before, identifying all the reasons that contribute to the top statement, that people prefer to buy in a shop.

8. Create as many analysis ladders of varying lengths (depending on the depth of the analysis) as you feel you need to really explore the challenge in full. So your page might end up looking something like this (see overleaf).

At the end of the exercise, you will have a much better understanding of all the different elements that contribute to your challenge, the root cause of some of the issues and the reason why some assumptions have been made. Now you can go on to write a much more informed brief.

The brief

Look around your business. What challenges do you currently face? To show the range of issues for which you can generate ideas with this creative process, I have recently worked with businesses to tackle the following challenges:

How to get more people to visit our website and purchase online

Customers don't know the web address	Customers prefer shop experience	Customers want to speak to an expert	Website is complicated to navigate
No advertising done recently	They want to touch and feel the products	To get advice on the product range	Too many clicks to get what you want
Customer base too diverse	Get a real idea of if the product is right for them	Range of products can be confusing	Products not sorted by function
Not targeting specific customer groups	So they make the right choice first time	Many products have only slight differences	
Not enough customer data			

- How to launch a new product

- How to get internal departments to work more effectively together

- How to knock the customers' socks off with amazing service

- How to bring the company vision and values to life for everyone in the business

- How to streamline key processes to save time and money

- How to work with a local charity in new and exciting ways.

When you are tackling a business challenge and trying to generate creative ideas, ensure you take time to assemble all the facts into a concise, informative brief. Once you have done the ladder analysis, use the insights it provided alongside other information you have in order to give a full, rounded picture of the challenge and the background to it. A great brief – one that brings the problem to life and gives insight into customers and the reason why it is being tackled – will help brains focus on the right elements of the challenge. It will provide enough information that it allows the group to concentrate on generating ideas rather than trying to deal with unanswered questions, yet gives the group permission to be as creative as they can possibly be.

Use this Challenge Checklist template to help you. Each point is explained in further detail below:

> **IDEAS SESSION**
>
> The challenge headline ....
>
> What is the background to this challenge?
>
> What have you tried before? What worked and what didn't?
>
> What are the key elements to this challenge?
>
> What do you want from the group?
>
> What is your Mind-Blowing Outcome?

The challenge headline

This headline must sum up the challenge that you are facing. I always find it useful to use 'How to …' as your starting point, as it helps you focus on the issue without making it seem impossible. Make the headline short, inspiring and precise and aim for no more than twenty words – many more will make it difficult to concentrate on the exact problem in hand. Don't be tempted to include several parts of the same challenge, or more than one challenge. The best challenge headlines are extremely single-minded; this helps keep the ideas on track as well as encouraging you to keep delving deeper for rich, creative solutions.

Don't make your challenge headline like this: *How to create an online resource for teenagers about healthy living.* It is short and to the point, but doesn't really excite or engage.

Or this: *How to create an online resource for teenagers about healthy living, as well as ideas for offline promotions that advertise the site and ideas for prizes for an online competition.*

This headline is almost a paragraph long. There are at least three different challenges stated; using this would result in the ideas being too scattered and vague.

Instead, create a headline more like this: *How to create an exciting online healthy living resource for teenagers that informs, inspires and creates a buzz.* This headline is focused on one challenge, but includes words such as 'exciting', 'inspires' and 'buzz' that will engage the group generating the ideas and give them more creative licence to come up with exciting and inspiring solutions.

Even if you are generating ideas by yourself, it is still a worthwhile exercise to write a brief in this way. The very process of composing it and organizing the associated information is an invaluable part of preparing your brain. It can also help you identify where you may need further insight or information to help you solve the challenge. Structuring what you know into this checklist, or a similar format, is a great way to start spotting where the real problem may lie and which particular directions may be ripe for exploring.

What is the background to this challenge?

This section is where you can include all the nuts and bolts of the issue you are facing – such as why this is a challenge for you, a little about the target market or people involved if relevant, and so forth. For example, using the challenge headline above, the background could read:

Teenagers are notoriously difficult to engage with on the subject of 'healthy living'. We need to get the key health messages out to them about: 1) eating and making smart food choices, 2) drinking and the dangers of alcohol and 3) the benefits and joy of exercise. Our research tells us that 96 per cent of teenagers own a mobile phone, 72 per cent of whom can use it to access the internet, and they spend on average 35 hours a week online.

What have you tried before? What has worked and what hasn't?

This question allows you to note down previous solutions and whether or not they have succeeded. Those in the former category could inspire the group to even better ideas, and stating those in the latter helps to prevent the group from revisiting old, unsuccessful ideas – this saves time and provides further focus.

For example: *We had an online presence within third-party sites, including government sites and a major supermarket, but these attracted only 2 per cent of our target market. A trial, on-off initiative at a local music festival involving healthy snack sampling and non-alcoholic cocktail shots proved very popular with 3,000 teenagers signing up to text info updates.*

What are the key elements to this challenge?

This is where the logistical issues are noted, such as budget, timings, resources etc. While it can be limiting to consider such matters too early, stating them within the Challenge Checklist can be useful. You can always decide to ignore the logistics at any point in the idea-generating process – giving yourself or the group permission to think beyond them.

 A great way to get people thinking in a highly creative way is to play with the scale of the budget – thus freeing your brain temporarily from the restraining logistics of the challenge. So you might ask the group: What would be your idea if you had £1 million to solve the problem? Or: What would be your idea if you had £1 to solve the problem? Both of these questions will provoke extreme answers – and probing into these further can often point you to the real gems of ideas.

What do you want from the group?

If you are generating ideas in a group, this is where you can be very specific about the type of ideas you are hoping for. You might say that you want big, ground-breaking ideas that will cause a stir. Or you could ask them for highly commercial ideas of which your competitors will be jealous.

What is your MBO: your Mind-Blowing Outcome?

Your Mind-Blowing Outcome describes what would happen if one of the ideas from the session was brilliantly successful. The key here is to state the outcome that you want in the most exaggerated, overblown and utopian way possible. This gives everyone who will be involved in the creative process (including you) permission not just to think big, but to think bigger than ever before. You should work together to create a compelling vision of what would happen if you came up with the most creative, amazing, successful solution to your challenge.

Using the healthy living challenge from above, your MBO should *not* be like this: *We would get 40 per cent of teenagers visiting the site*. As an ambition, it may be realistic, but it is definitely not inspiring or audacious.

Instead, you would put something like: *So many teenagers would flock to the site, and be so inspired by it, that we solve the obesity problem in a year. We would be on the front cover of every magazine, Jamie Oliver would call us geniuses and we could all retire with our new OBEs.* Realistic? Not really. But it will certainly inspire the group and give them licence to come up with some crazy, brilliant notions as a result.

These statements of wild aspiration are essential in assuring the group that there is no idea that they can come up with that will be too ridiculous. One of the most common barriers to creativity is self-censorship: the 'I can't say that, I will sound like an idiot' syndrome. But if you have already read out one of the most fantastical ideas, you have implicitly given them the go-ahead to be equally as outlandish. Because it is when the ideas start to leave the realms of the safe and the predictable that exciting creative things start to happen.

 If you are trying to solve a challenge single-handedly and a written brief seems too formal, a trick I often use is to just jot down the challenge headline and the Mind-Blowing Outcome on a Post-it, tuck that into my desk drawer and forget about it. I have, in essence, now briefed my subconscious. At some point, an idea will come to me about how to solve it, and often a number of ideas.

IF YOU REMEMBER ONE THING If you do not complete the full Challenge Checklist, the very least you should do in terms of preparation is to craft a powerful challenge headline and define your MBO (Mind-Blowing Outcome).

31

These two elements will provide focus and creative intent, which are crucial when you are generating ideas. However, the Challenge Checklist is a great way to get a group to understand the problem and provides a launch pad for some really creative thinking.

Incubation

Once you have briefed yourself or the group with all the relevant information, incubation begins – whether you like it or not. Your mind will automatically start addressing the challenge – or more specifically, your subconscious will. Luckily for us, the subconscious part of the brain starts to do all the hard work without us even having to think about it – our brains begin to process the information and work on ideas without our help. When I explain this in workshops, it can be met with scepticism. But how often have you had an idea pop into your head unbidden, seemingly from nowhere? That is your subconscious at work, pushing ideas and thoughts into your conscious brain so that you can act on them. It may seem a little uncontrollable, but you can help this process along by making sure that you put yourself in the best place to encourage ideas.

Neuroscience, and its investigations into why and how the brain creates new ideas and insights, is still really in its infancy. Professor Jonathan Schooler, professor of psychological and brain sciences at the University of California, is at the forefront of this research and one of his experiments deals specifically with the incubation stage of the creative process.

In this experiment, he asks volunteers to undertake a classic divergent thinking test (refer to page 7) using a house brick. They then all take a two-minute break. The first volunteer is asked to sit still and do nothing during the break. The second volunteer is asked to spend her break engaged in a non-demanding task (sorting Lego bricks into colours), while the third is asked to undertake a much more demanding task (building a model house from Lego). All three volunteers then take another divergent thinking test, still with the house brick, but with the stipulation that their ideas must be different from those they came up with previously.

The results show that those who are given a non-demanding task perform significantly better at the creativity test than the others – with the worst-performing set of volunteers being those who have to spend their break doing a demanding task. Professor Schooler speculates that while he cannot be entirely sure what is happening on a neurological level to facilitate this creative boost, it seems that engaging in a task that allows the brain to 'dip in and out' – i.e. switch back and forth between the task at hand (which takes little brain power) and the challenge (thinking about the house brick) 'stirs the pot and allows a certain kind of unconscious recombination that is particularly beneficial … for creativity.' Professor Schooler's work is showing that it is critical in the creative process that you let your mind wander – but be aware, as he puts it, that 'not all mind wandering is equal'.

A contemporary of Professor Schooler, Professor Rex Jung, assistant professor of neurosurgery at the university of New Mexico, is undertaking research into the neurological changes that happen in the brain during the creation of an idea or novel insight. His research has led him to the frontal cortex, an area of the brain whose function includes impulse control and judgement. At the moments where his volunteers report having insights, or flashes of inspiration, the activity of the frontal lobes dips momentarily – almost like a temporary sleep mode, which, he posits, allows ideas to flow much more freely from the subconscious into the conscious mind. Professor Jung explains that his research leads him to believe that people who naturally solve problems with insight have a lower baseline of frontal lobe activity – in other words, the brain is in a naturally more receptive and less self-censored state to receive ideas from the subconscious. There are ways to help the frontal lobes into a state whereby insights can come into consciousness more freely – activities, Professor Jung suggests, where the body is physically occupied while the brain is left to wander. He cuts the lawn when he needs to let his brain come up with ideas. But you don't need to carry a lawnmower around to have the same effect. Where do you have your best ideas?

I often ask the groups that I train in creative thinking skills this question and they write down where they have their best ideas, and where they feel they never come up with good ideas. Without fail, people tell me that locations like the bus, the shower, the bed, the train, the bath and the gym are among the best creative places for them. And the worst? Their desks. Which can prove problematic for a business that wants to be more creative – but more of that later.

So what do all these places that are not your desk have in common? I would suggest that they are places where you allow your mind to relax, to 'zone out' of all that effortful, conscious thinking, and let your subconscious flourish – where you are engaging in a spot of mind-wandering that suppresses frontal lobe activity and allows ideas to flow. They are places where you don't really have to 'think' at all.

THINK ABOUT IT
Consider these two questions now. Which locations inspire ideas for you? And which seem to squash your creativity? Use the space below to jot down the different environments that seem to help or hinder great ideas.

Places for great ideas	Places for no ideas

Looking at your list, I would guess that another factor that unites them is that they are places where other random, external stimuli can come into play. If 'walking the dog in the park' is one of the situations in which you have great ideas, you will be presented with a multitude of external stimuli – a bird swooping close to the ground, a kid in a red bobble hat, a funny-shaped cloud, a piece of litter scudding across the grass. All these things, and thousands more, will cross your path – but most of them without you consciously realizing. And, in my experience, this can be crucial for the creative process. This random stimulus is what Edward de Bono, a leading authority in the field of creative thinking, called 'provocation', and is part of what is known as a lateral thinking process.

Lateral thinking

Thinking laterally means that problems are solved using unexpected perspectives and by diverting from the more traditional, logical problem-solving approach. Our brains are brilliant at forming patterns – if you learn to open one door handle you can figure out how to open others, for example. Even if you come across a door with a slightly different handle, your brain will remember a pattern for 'doors with handles' to which the door in front of you conforms, so you can open it without learning how to do it all over again. This 'pattern thinking' is, of course, an essential skill for everyday life (imagine the time it would take if door-opening had to be learned anew every time you wanted to enter a room). But these patterns can be a real creativity killer, as you often approach a challenge with a pattern based on how this sort of problem was solved previously, blocking all new thoughts from the process.

Lateral thinking encourages the brain to look at a problem in a different, non-logical (and non-pattern) way, often by juxtaposing two or more random, disassociated thoughts or ideas together. So if you are tasked with reinventing the door, for example, a logical approach might take you down the thinking path: 'Logically, a door needs to move out of the way of the approaching person, so that the doorway is open and they can walk through it …' which might lead you to consider different ways of hinging a door, or creating an 'up and over' door. But I would suggest that these are still incremental door improvements. What if you brought in a totally random thought, such as … a biscuit (which just so happens to be sitting on my desk, waiting for me to finish this paragraph – a classic example of the effect of external stimulus). What if you consider a door *and* a biscuit? My brain jumped straight to the biscuit cutters I have in my kitchen drawer for making gingerbread men with my four-year-old. The brain will automatically try to combine these two thoughts – door and cookie cutter – and so I had an idea of a door that opens to the shape of each family member (a bit like in cartoons when someone is thrown through a wall, leaving a perfect outline of them where the wall once was). It would certainly be a novel way of creating a door – and with the added benefit of deterring unwanted intruders, particularly ones that are bigger than you. It would also let you know if you were eating too many of the aforementioned biscuits, which might be handy.

So lateral thinking helps you step outside of your usual patterns of thinking and consider your challenge in a new way, resulting in more creative and innovative solutions. It can be difficult to make the mental leap required to view your challenge from a new perspective, or allow a totally disassociated thought to inform your thinking, which is why random stimulus can be so important – it can force your brain into new ways of thinking. It literally disrupts an otherwise logical train of thought.

With people who are practised in the art of creativity, lateral thinking happens naturally. Their brains have become accustomed to making leaps out of a logical thought process and combining new thoughts together in novel ways. It happens without effort – ideas will simply pop into their conscious brain, as I have described above in the Incubation section (see page 32). However, for those who need more prompting to generate new ideas, you can deliberately introduce disassociated ideas into your thought process to help prompt lateral thinking to occur. It is also essential to be very purposeful in encouraging lateral thinking when a group of you are tackling a business challenge.

I use a tool that I have developed called Random Sparks to serve this purpose. In the diagram below, linear or logical thinking is interrupted by a Random Spark (for example, a biscuit), sending the thought process off in a new, tangential direction (the cookie-cutter door).

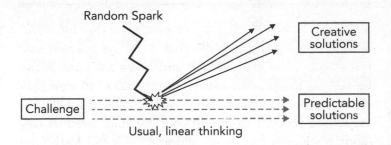

Usual, linear thinking

Random Sparks can be anything that acts as stimulus: a picture, a new thought, a sound, a word … almost anything that is not related to the task at hand will help change the way you think about it.

I worked with an online commercial archive business, who offered an extensive library of still and moving images and stock footage, from the very first images captured by rudimentary cameras to high-definition film. They wanted to become more of an online destination for prospective and existing customers, bringing in more creative professionals to a space where people explored their amazing archives rather than simply search for a required item, purchase and leave.

In this way, customers would learn more about what they offered, increasing repeat purchases and cross-selling other types of image.

Up until this point, internal brainstorms had thrown up ideas that were just incremental product or service improvements, such as changing the way people could search for what they wanted, and improving the layout of the online archive. All relevant ideas, but not the break-through ideas needed to attract a wider, more creative audience. These types of incremental ideas were typical of a logical way of thinking: here is the problem, this is what we have now, let's improve that in a small way to make it slightly better.

I ran a creative session with the team and used a lateral thinking approach to break their pattern thinking. It was crucial that I got each person in the room to think in a different way about their challenge to ensure that we got new, fresh ideas that were a leap away from where they started, not a small step. My first Random Spark was a pair of shoes – or several, to be precise. Each pair represented a type of customer that they wanted to attract; but I handed out the shoes without too much explanation, allowing each person to take the notion of 'shoes' and combine it with the challenge in any way they wanted. This immediately provoked a string of new ideas, such as online footprints from their competitors' sites to lead prospects to theirs, offering a free amazing image to 'shine up' the customer's website, and the idea of an online lounge where creatives could hang out. It was this last idea, of a virtual lounge, that made it to the ideas shortlist and eventually became an Inspiration Lounge.

Adopting a new angle can be more difficult than it at first seems. But it is imperative if a broad, mould-breaking range of ideas is going to be developed. Random Sparks that force people out of their viewpoints can be extremely helpful. There are a number of methods in the Creative Tool Kit section of the book that will help a group shift perspective to gain new insights and generate new ideas.

Where do I get Random Sparks from?
Random Sparks that create new thinking can come from absolutely anywhere. In the earlier example about deciding what to have for dinner, the Spark came from a walk to the shops. The trick is to be in a mental state where you are actively open to noticing things – this will help you to make the essential creative associations. It is easy to create a cache of Sparks for you or a group to use when you are thinking creatively. Collect objects and put them in a box – anything from a pine cone to a hair clip, toy car or hat. In the box you can also put pictures ripped from magazines, or old books from which you can pick a word. Then whenever you're in need of inspiration you can just pick a Spark from the box to help you think laterally about your challenge. If nothing

41

immediately springs to mind, don't just put it back in the box – be confident that the Spark will provoke a creative thought.

It is important to realize that your creative thoughts may not seem to be that promising at first glance. Using Random Sparks to help the creative process can create notions that are crazy, outlandish or just downright silly – and could be just the idea you need. It is essential that you suspend judgement about all the ideas that you generate, and only start the evaluation process later. It is often the case that a thought or idea that sounds ridiculous can be developed and turned into a practical solution. Let's not forget, there are many examples of ideas that were considered stupid – which then went on to create fortunes for the person responsible. In 2005, Alex Tew had the strange idea of selling a single pixel on his homepage for $1 to advertisers. Hands up who would have thought he could make $100, let alone over $1 million? Even though he admitted himself that his idea was 'quirky', he did just that. And businesswoman Sara Blakely had the crazy notion of creating shape-control tights that were footless. Every hosiery manufacturer that she approached with the idea indeed thought it was crazy – one lawyer she discussed it with even admitted that they thought she was part of a Candid Camera set-up. But Sara persevered and eventually created Spanx, now a $1 billion business. Not bad for a 'crazy' idea.

Once you have understood the challenge (the preparation and brief stage) it is very important to give yourself this incubation time to let the subconscious really get to work on solving the challenge. Ideally with incubation time, you allow yourself a few hours, a few days or even longer, *not* actively thinking about your challenge but letting your mind make lateral connections, using random stimulus that comes to you as you go about your day to help create new thinking. As we have noted, during the incubation time you will find yourself in situations and environments that help this process – from taking a walk to a soak in the tub. But in the business environment, there is rarely the time to accommodate this. If you are sitting with colleagues who are tasked with coming up with ideas, while a group trip to the showers might not be appropriate, there are plenty of tools (of which more later) that can help 'fool' the brain into the incubation process, and lots of ways to introduce those all-important Random Sparks that will lead you into the Illumination stage.

 Ideas will usually occur at the most inopportune time, when a pen and paper is far from handy – just as you're falling asleep, or in the shower, or any time your brain is in the optimum state to be creative. So as you get in the swing of letting your subconscious do the creative thinking, your biggest challenge will be remembering all the ideas you come up with.

Place notebooks strategically around your house, car or office – or perhaps instead you could download a voice recording app so that you can tell your phone about the great idea you've just had.

Illumination

This is the third stage of the creative process, where you have the light bulb moments. This is the result of the previous two creative stages. For the purposes of explaining the creative process, the Incubation period (where your brain is doing all the hard work while you do something else) and Illumination stage (where the ideas pop out) are separate and defined. In reality, these two stages can seem almost interchangeable. A train ride can provide great incubation time, and also result in an idea coming to you. You then walk to the office which offers another period of incubation, and by the time you reach the door, two more possible ideas have surfaced. When you are trying to solve a problem within a more structured time frame, the process will mimic this 'back and forth' movement between these two creative stages. You will perhaps consider a Random Spark, which will provoke a number of possible ideas. When you cannot come up with any more ideas, you can pick another Random Spark and the Illumination process will start all over again. Random Sparks essentially force your brain to create lateral connections to help it generate new ideas, and this can be repeated for as long as you have the energy to do so.

As Illumination occurs, ideas can come to you thick and fast. Whether inspiration strikes as you sit on the bus, or as a result of forcing a lateral thought with a Random Spark, you will have an idea. And this will then lead to another idea. And another. The ideas themselves will often inspire other ideas – sometimes a direct 'development' of one idea from other, sometimes something totally unconnected – and before you know it, you need another piece of paper to scribble them all down on.

At this stage there should be lots of questions. These questions may be provoked by a Spark from the Incubation stage, and are likely to be along the lines of: 'What if …?', 'Why …?' and 'Why not …?'. Imagine that your challenge is to get people to visit your website for product support rather than calling customer services. You pick a Random Spark: T-shirt. This provokes the question: 'What if we had our slogan on the front of our product?', leading to the idea of a sticker on every product, displaying your website address. Your next Random Spark is a bag of sweets, provoking the question: 'Why not give sweets to customers who use our website?'. This might not be practical, but could lead to the idea of incentivizing customers who visit your website with a money-off voucher or with loyalty points every time they log in. Questions like these will help make an association between your Spark and your challenge, and within this association lie the ideas.

Whether alone or in a group, it is important to capture these ideas. This will help you then build from one idea to the next, creating new ideas and options as you go. It is important that every idea is written down, even if you feel at that moment it is not of great value. You will return to all the ideas after this stage to evaluate them – trying to be critical and creative at the same time will simply not work: ideas will be rejected before you really have a chance to assess them and the idea generation will quickly dry up in the face of critical scrutiny.

 It's a good idea to nominate someone within the group to write down every idea that is generated, and preferably on a flip chart, so that the group can see the ideas as they are captured. The role of the 'scribe' is to write down the idea faithfully – there should be no adapting of the idea, no editing – which is why it is often useful to have a facilitator who does not contribute ideas, but leads the group and holds the flip chart pen. This way, there is no temptation for the scribe to make on-the-fly improvements to someone else's idea, or miss several contributions while trying to come up with ideas themselves.

In order to keep up the flow of ideas at this crucial Illumination stage and prevent premature judgement, it is essential that you disarm your inner critic.

Inner Critic

We all have an inner critic – that part of our brain that makes assessments and judgements about ideas and situations – and in a business environment, we rely on it daily to help us make quick decisions and the right choices. But newborn ideas are fragile: a snap decision about the value of a newly thought idea, allowing your conscious brain to label it 'silly' or without merit, can prevent a potentially great idea from even making it onto the flip chart.

Even if you are generating ideas alone, your own inner critic – while it may not actually tut at you – will stymie your creative output if you do not consciously turn it off. And in group situations, one of the biggest creativity killers is the fear of judgement by others, particularly more senior members of the group.

If you are in a group situation, prevent judging of ideas by setting out clear ground rules for the session before you start. Explain that there will be a time for evaluation, but it is not now. For persistent offenders I have shown them yellow and red cards with the threat of a forfeit for persistent offending (making the tea for everyone is usually enough of a deterrent).

There is also a common fear of looking silly in idea generation sessions. I often hear people contributing ideas by saying: 'This is a stupid idea, but what about …'. There are no stupid ideas in the Illumination stage of the creative process. I actively encourage 'stupid' ideas, not only by setting out an audacious goal in the Mind-Blowing Outcome to encourage people to think up ideas that are themselves outrageous, but by making it clear at the start of the session that crazy ideas are very much welcome.

 I was facilitating an idea generation session for a marketing agency who were trying to win a pitch for a company that sold cleaning products. Halfway through the session, one of the group said that she wished the cleaning products could help her lose weight. A floor cleaning fluid that could shed the pounds? Utterly ridiculous. Or was it? There was obviously a kernel of a great solution to the brief in this idea, as although when the idea was mooted it raised a few smiles (and a couple of eyebrows) it made it onto the shortlist for ideas to be developed. The idea was subsequently chosen as the best solution to take to the pitch and was presented as a marketing campaign that equated each household chore with the number of calories burned when you undertook that domestic job. So half an hour of vigorous vacuuming would burn 90 calories, while the same amount of time spent ironing would burn 30. It was proposed that on the label of each cleaning product, there would be a 'ready reckoner' to help consumers see how good cleaning could really be for their health. The pitch was won from that seemingly silly idea. It pays to go back and look long and hard at your silliest ideas, because they often contain creative gold dust.

Though it is possible, it can be difficult to come up with ground-breaking ideas by yourself, even with the add-ition of Random Sparks. It is said that a problem shared is a problem halved, but in idea generation, a problem shared is one where the possible solutions are multiplied. Collaboration can be key to creativity and the Illumination stage in particular can benefit from more than one brain, as this encourages what is known as 'idea building'.

Idea building

What will naturally happen in a group creative thinking session is that people will build on others' ideas. A person will offer one idea, and often someone else will say: 'Building on that, how about …' Each idea can spark several other ideas, tak-ing the germ of a thought in a different direction to the one that the originator might have conceived. People also tend to use classic creative thinking techniques on the fly when they are idea building, such as saying: 'So flipping that idea on its head, how about …?' Idea building is to be encouraged at the Illumination stage, and there is an idea building technique in the Tool Kit section (see page 113) of the book to help this.

Collaboration during the creative process in a business environment has another extremely beneficial side effect. People who are part of the idea generation process when a business challenge is being solved are significantly more engaged with the challenge than those people who are not involved. The process of contributing ideas and being part of the solution-making team gives people a stake in the challenge and a commitment to create a successful outcome. This can be commercially beneficial as it often circumvents any internal resistance to change and a 'not my problem' attitude that can be a barrier to success.

I was asked to bring together all the European marketing heads of a global retailer to come up with ideas for their summer promotion, which was to be offered to all the European franchises. Historically, take-up of these promotions had been around 10 per cent, as the franchised territories were not obliged to take part and run the customer promotions if they did not want to. For the first time, the heads of marketing were invited to the ideas session and were involved in the creative process of coming up with the idea for the summer promotion. The session explored the notion of families undertaking driving holidays and long-distance travel through Europe, and the group spent time putting themselves in their customers' shoes to help them come up with ideas that would really appeal. During the session hundreds of ideas were generated before one was selected, developed and implemented. That summer, franchise take-up of the promotion was around 90 per cent – because the marketing heads had helped to generate the ideas, understood their logic, and so opted into running the promotion as a result. Being engaged in the process in this way also meant that they were emotionally invested in making the promotion a success in their territory, as they felt it was 'their idea'. This sense of ownership of an idea and the subsequent stake in a successful outcome can reap real commercial and cultural advantages for a business.

Getting in the right frame of mind for the Illumination stage is important, whether you are on your own or in a group. Laughter and playfulness are critical ingredients in this process. Imagine sitting round a table, looking glumly at your colleagues, sighing heavily and then coming up with amazing ideas. It is just not going to happen, is it? Instead, you need to create a fun environment that will give visual cues to the group to have fun themselves. Encourage laughter – the most creative members of society, children, are said to laugh up to 400 times a day. But when you have mounting deadlines, your computer has just frozen and the kettle has broken, it can be a challenge just to raise a smile, and adults are reported to laugh only about fifteen times a day. Yet the endorphins released when you laugh and the accompanying decrease in stress hormones can have a hugely positive effect. Laughter in a group situation works to connect the group and diminish any threat, particularly the dangerous assumption that the senior people in the room are more important than others; it is a great leveller.

However, in a business context, there is no greater fun-killer than someone standing up and saying: 'Right, we are going to have some fun now.' Instead, choose a facilitator for the ideas session who will naturally encourage this outcome. You can also try using 'thinking toys' to encourage a sense of play – for example, Play Doh. Most people will want to have a play with it, and some studies have shown that engaging the fingers in a sensory activity stimulates the nerve endings that go directly to the brain.

 Gather a selection of items that could be useful thinking toys. You may not have a pot of Play Doh to hand – but what about Blu Tack? I also have used spiky rubber massage balls with groups and they are always popular. Even an unassuming paper clip can be a good stand-in, as people will inevitably bend and twist it out of shape while having a good think. Have a look around you and see what you can come up with to use as a thinking toy. Or, you can invest a little money and hand out Tangles – plastic loops made of several curved sections that can be twisted and turned in a variety of ways. The key to a thinking toy is that it should be easy to use without having to consciously think about what you are doing with your hands at all.

Using kids' toys and activities can also diminish our innate lack of confidence about being creative. In *Orbiting the Giant Hairball*, Gordon MacKenzie, a business creativity expert, described his research on this topic. He asked classes of six-year-olds how many of them were artists: all of them raised their hands. He then asked classes of ten-year-olds the same question, and about a third of them answered in the affirmative. Asking twelve-year-olds if they were artists resulted in only about one in 30 raising their hands. Our current education system, with its emphasis on right and wrong, and our culture of conformity, makes it hard to hang on to our creativity. Young brains that are naturally excellent at divergent thinking are eventually 'trained' to seek one right solution: a more creative approach is eschewed in pursuit of a singular, conformist answer. So giving people 'childish' activities to do can be a great way to release some of that pent-up creativity.

Imagine you are organizing an idea generation session in your business. Who would be a great facilitator and scribe? How would you encourage a sense of play and laughter?

What toys or props could you bring to the group to help this?

In summary, the Illumination stage is the heart of the creative process. It is worth spending time getting the setting for this stage right, whether you are on your own or in a group.

Evaluation

This final stage of the creative process is crucial, particularly within the commercial environment of a business. This starts the process of turning an idea, scribbled hastily on a flip chart, into reality. It is beneficial at this stage to revisit your brief – to remind yourself of what you set out to do and what your MBO was. There will often be fantastic ideas that actually do not answer the brief, and it is important from a business perspective that you are not seduced by these.

If you have come up with brilliant ideas that don't quite fit your brief, make sure to save them for a more appropriate time. In organizations with which I have worked I often suggest the creation of an 'ideas bank' – a central place where brilliant ideas that don't answer the current brief are kept, so that they can be recycled for another challenge. An ideas bank can be as simple as a notebook, or as advanced as an online, searchable repository.

The evaluation of your ideas should be a robust and considered process – you are about to make a decision that could change both your business and your bottom line, so it's imperative that an idea is well assessed.

It can be tempting to dismiss ideas on a hunch, or because you personally don't like them. And conversely, I have seen far too many ideas pursued by the person who created them because it's always tempting to think that our own suggestions are the best. But this is the time for logical, linear thinking. Now is the time to leave divergent thinking behind and adopt convergent thinking as the best evaluation tool.

 Convergent thinking is deductive, critical thinking, bringing information together in an attempt to find a single clear solution to a problem.

The best way to ensure that you can judge your ideas properly is to spend some time thinking of the right evaluation criteria – things that will prevent your own subjective opinions from ruling your head. These criteria could include:

- Does it answer the brief, deliver the desired outcomes and fit with my MBO?

- Will it fit the budget?

- Will it fit the timescales?

- Will it be achievable with current available resources?

- What are the risks of implementing this idea?

- What are the risks of not implementing this idea?

- How will customers react to it?

- How will competitors react to it?

- Will it be profitable?

- Will it enhance our brand and our positioning?

This is by no means an exhaustive list, and not all of these evaluation questions will be relevant, but it is an essential part of the process. So, let's take the challenge mentioned previously about how to encourage customers to visit your website for product support rather than calling customer services. There may be a number of potential ideas from all those that you generated that you wish to explore further. For example, one of these shortlisted ideas could be placing a sticker on all your products that directs customers to the support section of your website.

Does it answer the brief, deliver the desired outcomes and fit with my MBO? This is where you should check back on your brief. If the MBO was that 100 per cent of customers used the website, could you see the product stickers achieving this?

Will it fit the budget? This evaluation criteria may take a little time to work out accurately – consider the cost of the sticker design and manufacture, as well as that of applying the stickers, and possibly developing the website to accommodate increased traffic and more customer questions.

Will it fit the timescales? Again, in order to accurately evaluate the sticker idea, you will need to analyse the time needed for each stage to ensure it would be achievable within your deadlines.

Will it be achievable with current available resources? Who has the right experience to manage the project internally? And external resources – such as printers or website developers – have to be considered too.

What are the risks of implementing this idea? This is not just about financial risks. Explore as many different aspects as you can, such as to the products – is there a risk in putting stickers on products? What if the stickers leave a messy residue? What are the risks if the sticker stays on the product once it is being used? Will it start to peel, or the colour run, or make the product look untidy?

What are the risks of not implementing this idea? This evaluation criterion is about the risk of doing nothing. What would happen? If you did not sticker the products and most customers continued to call customer services, what would the risks be, financially and otherwise? It can be useful to compare these risks of doing nothing against the risks involved with implementing the idea, as it helps to put the risk of a new idea in perspective.

How will customers react to it? You may know what a lot of your customers would feel if they purchased one of your products with a sticker on it. If you don't, part of your evaluation might be to go and find out, through customer feedback. Does their reaction show the idea in a positive or negative light? If feedback shows that they think a sticker cheapens the product, does this make the idea a non-starter?

How will competitors react to it? It is useful to consider what impact, if any, your idea will have on your competitors. Big, disruptive ideas can scare the competition – or leave them standing – which could work in your favour. Stickers on products probably won't have them quaking in their boots, but could they capitalize on your decision by positioning themselves as the company that encourages human interaction with customer service people rather than a website? How would that affect you?

Will it be profitable? It is important to carry out projections on the idea, including set-up, manufacture and implementation and any ongoing costs, as well as cost savings or direct profit that will potentially occur.

Will it enhance our brand and our positioning? This can be a tricky one to evaluate with accuracy, but is important nonetheless. What impact will stickers on products have on your brand? If you are a high-end technology brand with a highly engineered product range, do you really want a sticker plastered over your products? You could be doing potential damage to how customers perceive your brand. If your brand positioning is all about beautiful design, would the sticker idea work for or against this? Apparently the latter, but this does not mean that the idea should necessarily be shelved. The essence of the idea may work with all the other criteria, so it is worth exploring ways to overcome this hurdle. Perhaps it is not a sticker after all, but a beautifully designed tag with a QR code (a matrix barcode that can be scanned by mobile phones) on it to drive people to the website. It could even be a mini USB stick with the website address loaded onto it. You may find that in the process of evaluating an idea, it morphs into a new incarnation that will better fit with your evaluation criteria. Don't be afraid of this – it is all part of the creative process. Take the new, improved idea and evaluate that one. It may be just what you need to persuade your customers to seek their support online.

At this stage it helps to have several people doing the evaluation – and if possible, some of those should be people who were not involved in the creative process, as having fresh eyes on an idea is key. There are also a number of great evaluation tools that can make this process very straightforward, and these can be found in the Creative Tool Kit section of this book.

The structure of an idea generation session

So now you know the theory of the four stages of creativity, how do you translate that into a workable idea generation format within your business? Because it is all very well understanding that a brain needs a period of incubation time, but how practical is it to let half of your team wander around a forest or go home and sit in the bath until inspiration strikes?

The best way to harness these techniques is to run creativity sessions around your chosen challenge. You can plan these in any way you want, but here is a session structure based on the key stages of preparation, incubation, illumination and evaluation that can take as little as 90 minutes. The more time you dedicate to an ideas session, the better it can be, and I advise no less than 90 minutes if you are working in a group of six or more. Generally I find it best to limit the group to no more than eight or nine to avoid people's contributions being 'lost' among a crowd of more vocal participants.

Prior to the session, you should complete the preparation stage by gathering all the relevant information and filling out the Challenge Checklist as detailed previously. You should also prepare a number of Random Sparks in advance. This will ensure that you have enough creative stimulus to encourage the group to think from different perspectives. As I have discussed, a Random Spark will shift the direction of the ideas to new ground and re-energize the group with fresh inspiration.

Icebreaker

An icebreaker should be a fun question that is easy for everyone in the room to answer. The idea of an icebreaker is to relax everyone and get their focus into the room, leaving behind whatever email, conversation or project had their attention a moment ago. You can relate the icebreaker to the challenge, but it is not essential. It's very important that everyone takes it in turn to give an answer, so that each person has 'air time' right at the beginning of a session. Otherwise, someone who has not contributed anything and has not had their voice heard will become increasingly reluctant to speak up.

Good examples of icebreakers would be asking what people's favourite Christmas present was as a kid, or what their favourite journey is. These are easy questions for people to answer because you are not asking for invention, you are asking for recollection. The most important thing is to choose questions that nobody could feel nervous about answering. Their answers may also generate laughter and help to relax the group further, and if you're really lucky they could even provide some food for creative thought.

Even if your icebreaker is not related to your business challenge, it can be good practice to capture the essence of the response from each person on the flip chart. For example, in the Christmas present icebreaker above, you might jot down 'train', 'record player', 'doll that wees' and 'bike'. Believe it or not, these will make great Random Sparks later in your session, and this way you have already got a whole range of Random Sparks at your fingertips, that will already be in your team's heads subconsciously.

There are more examples of icebreakers in the Tool Kit section of the book.

Ground rules

Draw up a shortlist of ground rules for the group to abide by during the session. This may seem a little autocratic but it is essential to give the group a collective way of behaving. It is up to you to decide which ground rules are appropriate for your ideas sessions – and your business – but often mine will include:

- All mobile phones switched to silent.

- No judging. At this stage all ideas are good ideas. (This rule also includes no positive judging, as validating an idea with 'Oh, great idea' and not doing so to another is still a judgement).

62

- No questions. Questions stop the flow of the session so should be discouraged. This is the reason why it is important to take time to prepare a great brief – a successful brief is concise and leaves no questions unanswered.

- Raise ideas with the preface 'I wish …' or 'How to …'. I encourage people to use this linguistic format when giving their answers, as it's a great way to stop the natural tendency to waffle – explaining where they got the idea from, how it might work in detail and why they think it's great. Without this format, an idea is often delivered like this: 'I was just thinking about the idea of a magnet and that got me thinking about sticking things … so how about an idea around putting a sticker on with the website address? We could have a funny message on it, or a product tip, and we could probably also have one on the box, we would just have to work out how to get the stickers on the products in the first place, but it would work, as the customer would have to notice the sticker to peel it off …' And so on and so on. None of this supplementary information is needed at this stage; all the group needs to hear is a concise idea nugget that can be communicated in one short sentence: 'How to have the website address on a sticker on each product.' Or, if there is a secondary idea as part of the main idea, it could be: 'How to have the website address on a product sticker that includes a handy product tip'.

It can be difficult at first to use the 'I wish...' and 'How to...' format when expressing ideas but it only takes a little practice for it to feel natural. Think of an idea about how to improve your daily commute. Got one? Now try to express this idea in the concise format. So, I might think that a neck massage would help my daily commute, as I get quite stressed with all the late-running trains that play havoc with my tight schedule. But rather than say all that, I only voice the important bit: the idea. I would say: 'I wish I could have a neck massage on the train' or 'How to get a neck massage at the end of my commute.' Now try expressing ideas in this format for these other challenges:

- How to have a better work/life balance
- How to become a better cook
- How to do something positive for the environment every day.

It is helpful to write the ground rules on a piece of flip chart paper and have them on display throughout the session as a reminder to the group.

The brief
The facilitator should read the prepared brief to the group – this will have all the information that they need to start generating ideas. It should not be ten pages long, or the

group will switch off long before you finish reading it. If you can keep it to a single A4 page you will keep their attention throughout. When the brief has been read, the challenge headline should be written on a large piece of paper and pinned up for the duration of the session – as the facilitator can refer to this headline from time to time to refocus the group.

Initial ideas

In this part of the session the group should start to contribute ideas and the facilitator should write them down. The first ideas may be a little 'thin', because these will more often than not be the obvious things that people have thought of while hearing the brief. I have never run a creative session where the final selected idea comes from this initial set of thoughts, but it is nonetheless important that these are all captured so that the group can dismiss them, or build on them and move to more fertile creative ground. The group will soon lose momentum as these initial ideas are exhausted, which is the facilitator's cue to move on to the next part of the session.

Random Sparks and more ideas

When the group is starting to run out of ideas, the facilitator should introduce a Random Spark. This is the stimulus that provokes lateral thinking, which will produce new inspiration. Without it, the group is likely to explore the same type of ideas again and again, in typical 'pattern thinking' behaviour. For the first Random Spark, you could use the material collected from the icebreaker. So, if you are solving the challenge of how to improve your daily commute, you could ask the group to consider the notion of a 'record player' and how it would improve their commute. This Spark will encourage everyone to make connections, some more random than others. Naturally, the brain will respond to 'record player' with a thought – anything from 'music' to 'old technology' to 'mahogany'. The brain then sets to work forging an idea from a combination of that thought and the challenge. This is a facsimile of the Incubation process I described earlier, but with a more structured approach.

Everyone thinks differently, so from one Random Spark – the record player – you could get very different ideas. For example, one participant might immediately think of music, and say: 'I wish I had a playlist on my iPod to relax and inspire me in the mornings.' For another, record players might remind them of old technology – their idea might be: 'I wish my train was supersonic so it took me five minutes to get to work.' A third person might think of mahogany and come out with: 'I wish I could travel in style, and get upgraded once a week for being a loyal customer.'

One record player: three very different ideas.

The ideas that are provoked by a Random Spark may seem totally unrelated to the Spark that was presented for consideration. This is as it should be, and no explanation of seemingly unconnected ideas should be asked for — it is utterly irrelevant and will slow the creative flow. All the group should be concerned with is the great ideas that have come from the Random Spark.

Almost anything can be a Random Spark. Everyday objects, words from books, images ripped from magazines, or even a question, a celebrity or a profession – the possibilities are endless. The only criterion is that a Spark must be something that can jolt the group's thinking off its current track and onto a completely different one.

Once you have introduced a Random Spark, let the ideas keep coming. As described earlier, the group will instinctively build on ideas that come from others, so the ideas themselves become stimuli for further creativity. So having heard the idea about a five-minute commute, someone might add: 'How to make my spare room into my office', which totally flips the challenge on its head, and possibly the best way to improve the daily commute.

The Ideas–Random Spark–Ideas–Random Spark format makes up the main part of the session and in 90 minutes, you could use between two and six different Random Sparks to keep the group's creative juices flowing. Focus on the quantity of ideas, not the quality – the aim is to create as large a pool of ideas as possible. With the format outlined here, general discussion and development of ideas should be kept to a minimum to allow the group to maintain the momentum of creating new thoughts.

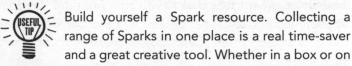 Build yourself a Spark resource. Collecting a range of Sparks in one place is a real time-saver and a great creative tool. Whether in a box or on a shelf, have a dedicated place to keep Sparks that you come across. Magazine images, old toys, electrical cable, a book, a rubber duck, a wooden spoon – anything could be a great Spark to use in a session. Keep it updated to keep your Sparks fresh; it's important that they're inspiring for you too.

What if there is one person in the group who is not contributing?

I have occasionally run sessions where there is someone not really contributing ideas. There could be several reasons for this, but I tend to respond by introducing a new Spark – it might be that they simply cannot come up with an idea at that time and a new Spark will hopefully reignite their creativity. It can also help to do a 'round robin', where you ask each person in turn for an idea – that way, they have to participate and get back in the flow of contributing ideas.

There are further examples of Random Sparks in the Tool Kit section of this book.

The evaluation snapshot

At the end of each ideas session, it is a valuable exercise to get the group to do a first-stage evaluation of ideas and create an initial shortlist. I call this an evaluation snapshot.

The evaluation snapshot

The group are asked to select the three ideas from the session that they feel best deal with the challenge headline. This is not meant to represent critical analysis, but is a first-stage assessment of where the strongest ideas may lie.

The group will have now been witness to all the ideas generated (which could be well over 100 in a 90-minute session), and they will have had time to really consider the challenge from a multitude of perspectives. Remind the group of the challenge headline (because a great idea that does not answer the brief should not make it to the short-list, but will definitely make it into the ideas bank) and give the group five or so minutes to review all the ideas; it is useful to have the flip chart sheets pinned up around the room for this. Instruct everyone to pick three ideas each – only one of which may be their own.

FAQ

What's this all about?

Why ask each group member to pick only one of the ideas that they came up with? Because we naturally think our own ideas are the best – we are emotionally invested in them and highly subjective about them. Those who consider themselves the 'ideas people' often baulk most at this request. I ran an ideas session with a business where one senior person argued with me about not being allowed to pick more than one of his own ideas as he felt that those solutions had, in his words, the most potential. On my insistence – because there were a whole host of great ideas on the sheets that were not his, and there was no good reason for me to change a rule I know works – he seemingly acquiesced. When it came to giving me his selected three ideas, I spotted that he had in fact chosen two that were his own, such was his belief that his ideas were better than the others. I gave him the choice to pick again, or stick with two ideas. Asking that people choose at least two that came from someone else helps them review the pool of ideas in more detail and with objectivity. And if their ideas are really that amazing, they will be selected for the shortlist by others in the group anyway.

This evaluation stage is not about discussion. It is important that the group members come to their own decisions about the strongest ideas, otherwise there may be undue influence from some people over others – you don't want everyone to feel that they have to pick the boss's idea. Get the group to write each idea down on a piece of paper so that they commit to their choices. Then you can ask each person in turn to tell the group which ideas they feel best answer the challenge. There will be some that several people have picked: this is what you are looking for, as this consensus can steer you towards the potential solution.

So that is the structure of the ideas session, whether it is 90 minutes or a full day. If you are running a longer session, you can also think about re-energizing the group with physical Random Sparks, such as changing seats or throwing a ball to one another while saying a word inspired by a Spark. This will literally get the blood flowing and help boost brain power. For more tips on jump-starting inspiration, look at the Tool Kit section of the book.

To summarize the format:
- Icebreaker
- Ground rules
- Brief
- Initial ideas
- Random Spark
- Ideas
- Random Spark
- Ideas
- Evaluation snapshot

The ideas that you will have as an outcome of this process are often still embryonic. Occasionally, ideas do pop up that require little further development, but more often, further time is required to develop and flesh them out. This process may seem long-winded, but I have been in ideas sessions where idea development takes place simultaneously with idea generation. What tends to happen is that the pace slows to a crawl, as everyone's brains try to flip from thinking creatively and expansively to critically and logically and back again. It just does not work, and the end result is a few, weak creative ideas that are poorly developed. It is a much more effective approach to ring fence the idea generation process using the format I have outlined above, and then reconvene, possibly with a smaller group of people, to start to develop and evaluate the preferred ideas.

Other things to consider for the idea generation session

Think about the environment in which you hold the session. Ideally, the group will sit on comfortable chairs or sofas without a table in front of them – because the less like 'work' it feels, the more relaxed and receptive to thinking in new ways the group will be – although this is not always easy in a work environment. However, it will always be possible in a business that puts creativity at its heart, as creating the right environment is critical in encouraging ideas. You can read more about this later on in the book.

Another important factor to consider in a successful ideas session is what I call 'fresh eyes'.

Fresh eyes refers to someone who is not connected or involved with the challenge in any way and will bring a new perspective to the challenge.

The original challenge may have arisen from the sales team – however, if you populate your ideas session solely with sales people, you will get a high degree of similar thinking. You need to include people who are not experts. In fact, the less they know the better. Some of the most successful sessions that I have run have included staff from reception, IT and admin support, as these people tend to bring a naivety to the challenge that is critical for new inspiration.

I facilitated an ideas session for a children's shoe retailer, whose challenge was to come up with a great promotional idea for the new school term that would engage kids and get them excited about buying shoes. In the session was a Mac operator who was usually not involved in this part of the process, alongside the more usual suspects of the client account team. It was this section of the group who contributed more fully, as this was very much their 'territory'. However, after making the Mac operator feel comfortable by using occasional round robins so that she had sufficient air time and voiced a number of ideas, she seemed to be getting into the swing of it. I handed round cards, which each depicted a different pair of shoes – court shoes, builder's boots, clowns shoes with a pom-pom on the toe, ballet pumps, running shoes and so on. Each person was asked to consider the shoes on their card and was asked how these shoes could help to create a great new promotion. A number of people contributed ideas, such as giving away a free ballet lesson with each purchase, and having building toys in store to entertain the kids. And then the Mac operator looked up from her card and said: 'I wish I could be in someone else's shoes.' This idea ultimately became the promotion: that kids could win a day in their hero's shoes. Who wouldn't want to be in David Beckham's shoes for a day?

As well as including fresh eyes, you should also look to create as much diversity as possible within the group, for example in terms of age and background, to encourage a good range of contributions.

Things to avoid in idea generation sessions

Leading a group of people is a skill that takes time and effort to execute well, let alone master. But there are a few key things to watch out for when you are running a session – things that I have seen happen in creative sessions that squash the good ideas (and the will to live) of the people in the room.

- Identify people in your business who will try to dominate the session with their own ideas. Senior staff are often particularly bad at this! They will often already 'know' the best solution and this conviction can sometimes be accompanied by an insistence on judging other ideas. This is the quickest way to ensure no one dares contribute even the most sensible-sounding idea. The best way around this is to leave these people out of the brainstorming session entirely. Instead, invite them in at the evaluation session, where their focus on critiquing can come into its own.

- Don't spend the entire session doing 'round robin' exercises so that everyone has exactly equal air time. Instead, allow the group to fire off each other, building on other people's ideas and taking the ideas in whichever direction they want. In this way, the session will have a real sense of momentum and energy.

- When ideas seem to be going off track and the group starts moving away from the challenge at hand, don't be too quick to rein them in. Wild, outlandish ideas are what you should be listening out for – sometimes a kernel of inspiration capable of transforming the whole challenge will be hidden in these ideas.

- Don't let people take notes. Pads and pens are for doodling and sketching – note taking will withdraw that person from the dynamic of the group. The facilitator will capture the ideas, so no note-taking is required from the group.

- Make sure idea generation sessions are held regularly – as with everything, practice makes perfect. Task staff with identifying things in the business that could be improved or changed, get everyone involved with sessions by holding them weekly and get everyone to give their creative muscles a regular workout.

2. Growing a Culture of Creativity

The only thing that can't be commoditized is creativity.
Creativity is what will separate the winners from the
also-rans in the emerging world of business.

Josh Linkner, *Disciplined Dreaming*

In the introduction, I looked at why creativity is so crucial in business and the reasons why it gives a business a distinct commercial advantage. It is worth stressing that it is not only businesses that sell products that should embrace creativity; innovations in service are equally as critical. Take Direct Line. In the early 1980s, taking out car insurance meant visiting a high street broker who took all your details and then sent them off to insurance companies for quotes. That is, until Peter Wood set up Direct Line, which used databases and phone operators to bypass the brokers and offer competitive quotes over the phone. This creative idea changed the face of the insurance industry and helped grow Direct Line into one of the biggest car insurance companies in the UK.

But just running the occasional idea generation session does not make a business creative. It is essential that a business is shaped by creative intent from the inside out, not only embracing regular ideas sessions, but putting creativity at the centre of everything the business does. As Tom Kelley notes in his book about his consistently innovative design company IDEO, *The Art of Innovation*, it is such a creative business because 'it is a blend of methodologies, work practices, culture and infrastructure'. In this chapter, I will look at some of the ways in which businesses can foster a culture of creativity, putting ideas at the heart of what they do and how they do it in order to reap the rewards.

Taking it to heart

Does your business have a set of organizational values? Most companies have devised them at some point, but they are often found languishing in the back of someone's desk drawer in a folder ironically marked 'Important'. Yet they really are important, as they form one of the foundation stones of an organization. Creating a meaningful set of values for your business gives the people in it a real sense of what is expected of them and a guide to the behavioural norms to be encouraged that will lead to your business mission being fulfilled.

So what do your organizational values say about you?

Grab a Post-it note or flip chart and jot down words related to creativity and having ideas. What did you come up with? My initial words included curious, questioning, challenging, risk-taking, exploring, expansive, collaborative ... but there is no definitive list.

Do any of these words, or words like them, appear as part of your organizational values or mission statement?

If your organizational values do not represent the spirit of the creative notion, how can your business be expected to be creative? How will people know how they are supposed to achieve the mission that has been set for them, whether this is to bake the best loaf in the world, to be the biggest retailer in the world, or to bring a smile to every customer's face? Organizational values act as signposts for behaviour and attitude and so it is imperative that if you are trying to prioritize creativity, your values reflect this. Your business mission may change as your business evolves: the values will remain constant.

Organizational values are part of a virtuous circle of business performance. Let's say one of yours is 'Using creativity every day to delight our customers'. The performance circle would look like this:

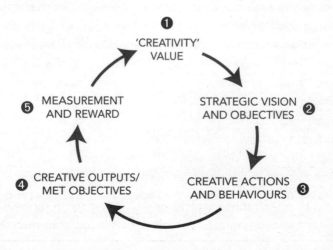

The creativity value you can see in the diagram at position number 1 of 'using creativity every day to delight our customers' (the message to the organization) informs and supports the strategic vision (number 2) which in turn defines the strategic objectives of the business. These objectives direct creative action (number 3), which in turn leads to creative outputs (number 4) – new ideas that then lead to innovation – that fulfil these objectives, and these in turn are measured and rewarded (number 5). The success of creative outputs subsequently reinforces the creativity business value, and the virtuous circle begins again.

It is the business leader's responsibility to make the business vision and values live and breathe. I have worked with too many organizations where the senior team has a clear notion of what the business stands for; yet when asked, the rest of the staff have no idea what their collective vision is supposed to be. It takes consistent application to drive the vision and values through every part of the organization. They should be woven into everything the business does, from new staff inductions, through staff communications, to how staff performances are measured. It also takes work to ensure that every person in the business understands how to demonstrate and work by these values every day. It is all very well letting everyone know that you have a creative approach to business – but what does that actually mean? How does the receptionist, the sales representative or the operations manager demonstrate this in their job?

I worked recently with a digital marketing agency who realized that their vision was languishing in a drawer somewhere and needed to be a much more vital part of the business, as they felt they were lacking momentum and needed to re-engage the staff with the business and its goals. I designed a workshop that gave every member of staff the chance to really understand what the vision, which was all about creating products that made customers happy and confident, meant to them as an individual, and what it meant in relation to what they did. We spent time exploring how every area of the business – from the physical environment to the business processes to the end product – could better embody that vision. The group was split into task forces, and each tackled one of these areas, looking at how they could make it reflect more closely the values of the business. So the environment task force redesigned the office layout, creating new 'ideas exchange' areas away from the desks that encouraged collaboration, which would create better ideas and give people more confidence that the business was working. The processes task force looked anew at the process and re-engineered it to take out bottlenecks to make people more confident that their work goals could be achieved. Engaged anew by a sense of purpose and collective direction, and enthused by the fact that they themselves had been responsible for the ideas about how to make improve the business in which they worked, the task forces set about making radical changes to their business so that they could truly live their creative vision.

A business vision not only has to be shared, but also has to filter down into the strategic imperatives for the organization. Creativity should be part of these strategic goals, so that, for example, each department or team leader has specific responsibilities for innovation and is measured regularly against agreed objectives (see the 'Measure It' section of this chapter on page 110 for more information on this). By doing this, the business will be consistently innovating, whether that be through process, operations, service or products – and this is the key to creating a long-term competitive advantage. Innovate to put yourself ahead of your competitors, and innovate like crazy to keep yourself there. Gillette are a great example of this. They regularly make their own shaving products obsolete with continual innovation that makes the last model – along with competitors' products – redundant. After all, who wants to shave with a razor that has only two blades, when you can shave with a razor that has five?

When you embark on the journey to make your business more creative, it may be helpful to put together a creative charter – which, of course, can be alternatively named to suit your business. This is a set of guidelines that will outline your approach to being a creative business, to help everyone within it understand what is expected of them in terms of attitude and approach. It is simply an extension of one of your business values, but it can be a worthwhile exercise to create a charter too, as it will not only be a clear definition of creativity within the commercial context, but can also can be a great way to show employees, clients and potential clients that you mean creative business. Work with the business to shape your charter in an appropriate way – here is just one example of what a creative charter could look like:

Ideas Inc.: Our Creative Charter

Share our creative vision and demonstrate our creativity every day.

Do things that encourage and celebrate great ideas.

Every idea has value. If we can't see it, we need to look a bit harder.

Ideas might not work first time. Don't give up. Adapt, tinker, tweak, turn it on its head to see if it works.

Being a creative business might not be the easiest path. But it is the most inspiring and commercially beneficial one, and the view is great.

It is imperative that a creative vision such as this is created collaboratively with the business. I find that this gives a much greater chance of engendering and sustaining cultural change. The charter should be constantly shared with the whole business, just as I have discussed with the values, to reinforce that it is essential to what you do and how you do it. And this extends to recruitment too: recruit people with a creative spark who will cultivate that in others, and make the business's creative vision clear to them.

Taking the creative lead

As a business leader – or a department head or team leader for that matter – it is up to you to embody the creative values of your company and lead by example. It is all very well having creativity in your strap line, on your T-shirts or on your home page, but unless you are living these values yourself the atmosphere of creativity will die and the ideas will soon fizzle out.

> *A creative leader isn't somebody who tells people what to do. They create the conditions and culture where everybody can have ideas.*
> Ken Robinson, London Business Forum 2011

THINK ABOUT IT

What do you do to encourage your business or team to be more creative? What actions and behaviours do you demonstrate that reinforce the message?

There are many ways in which people can be empowered to think more creatively. What opportunities do your people have to come up with ideas to improve or change your business or industry? Google famously has its '20 per cent time' where each employee has space in their schedule to play around and investigate new ideas. LinkedIn gives its engineers time to innovate in the 'InCubator', offering 30 to 90 days away from their day-to-day work to develop ideas into products. Apple has a similar programme called 'Blue Sky'. What do these companies have in common? A focus on ideas. Giving people time to get away from their desks and think expansively and in depth about a business challenge – whether it is one that has been given to them or one that they have identified themselves – speaks volumes about the leader's commitment to creativity. While you may feel it isn't practical to lose staff from their desks for substantial periods of time, consider the benefits – not only will you be fully exploiting your brain capital, you will be generating a constant flow of ideas into your business and hugely boosting staff morale and loyalty.

Another, less extreme way to build creativity into your business is to schedule regular idea generation sessions. If you got a group of people together every month – with a tray of cakes, fruit and drinks – and spent a couple of hours tackling a business challenge using the format that has been described previously, what message would you send out to your business? And, for that matter, your customers?

I work with a media organization that recognizes the importance of putting ideas at the heart of what they do. While they do not give their staff scheduled away time on an individual basis, they run quarterly away days with staff. In each of these sessions, a business challenge is presented to the staff, who work in small, cross-departmental teams to explore the challenge, generate a huge number of ideas and present their strongest solution to the rest of the business. A small group is then selected to work on implementing the idea in the next quarter, and their involvement and the change that they effect are all noted as part of their staff reviews. Staff feel valued that they have this regular opportunity to contribute to the 'bigger picture' of the business in which they work, and feedback has shown that they appreciate having their voice heard. It also gives them a useful insight into where the business is focused, which helps to add context and clarity to their contributions. Needless to say, the organization is constantly evolving and keeping well ahead of its competitors.

By behaving in this way, business leaders empower people to challenge the status quo, ask questions and have great ideas. I will talk further about how this success can be measured later in the chapter, as this is an essential part of putting creativity at the centre of your business. The leader of a business that values ideas is one that will invest time, money and resources in ideas, who knows that every member of staff is capable of having great ideas and who will always reward creativity.

Inspire your people

Open pretty much any book about being more creative and you will come across a sage piece of advice central to having great ideas: do something different. Take a different route to work, pick up a magazine about something you know nothing about, visit an art gallery, make some cupcakes, see a new film ... anything that will jolt your brain out of its mundane, everyday routine and create 'new' thinking.

If you are striving for a creative business it is important that you create inspiring and thought-provoking experiences for your staff. It might seem unproductive on a superficial level, but all these novel experiences can be the lifeblood of creativity, as they introduce Random Sparks into the working day and allow people to juxtapose ideas from unrelated areas with the workplace or challenge at hand, resulting in fresh insights and new ideas. I know of companies that give opportunities to learn subjects like cooking or photography as part of their training programme. Such topics seem irrelevant to the core business activity, but they are invaluable in giving people the chance to exercise their creative muscles. Encouraging creativity is all about new experiences, so going on a photography course can feed positively into someone's job by giving the person new experiences that can provide inspiration for their business challenges, as well as helping to make creativity a bigger part of their life in general.

Collaboration is king

As previously stated, there should be an expectation within a business that everyone contributes ideas, to really make the most of its brain capital. An organization will never grow and sustain a culture of creativity if this only occurs in small, isolated pockets of the organization.

Emphasize your creative intent for the business by identifying those people who could, informally or formally, champion creativity. You could, for example, nominate these people as Creative Champions, Ideas Ambassadors, Bright Sparks or whatever you wish, and make them responsible for any number of activities that will promote a creative culture, such as:

- Bringing people together for idea generation sessions

- Being trained to facilitate ideas sessions expertly

- Collecting challenges from the business to put through the idea generation format

- Getting involved in harvesting ideas from across the whole business (more of this later)

- Arranging PR for your creative initiatives.

As I have mentioned before, it is important to get fresh eyes on a challenge, and collaborating with other departments and job functions is a great way to do this.

Input from people in other departments, who are not as close to the problem as you are, is a huge asset when it comes to breaking assumptions and creating new ideas. It also allows people to bring their experience to a new context, which is another fertile ground for inspiration.

Another excellent way to promote collaboration across a business is to create a 'knowledge bank' of your staff.

Knowledge bank

This is a database of people that is much like a staff directory, with names, addresses, contact numbers and so on, but instead of the usual dull facts it contains a summary of something much more valuable: their experience.

When you have a challenge to tackle, picking the right brains for the creative job is half the battle. So, the knowledge bank entry for Joe Bloggs might contain the industries that he has worked in (print, retail, mining); the companies and clients he has previously worked with and for; his hobbies (motorbikes, extreme mountain-biking, crochet) and any other specialist skills (black belt in karate). Using a bank of such detailed profiles, you can assemble a group that includes a diverse range of experiences, backgrounds and interests, both relevant and disassociated – your fresh eyes – for the task at hand.

For larger businesses, another initiative that can encourage collaboration across the entire business is to create a role swap. In the same way as many management training

programmes have the trainee spend time in every department to ensure a thorough understanding of every part of
the organization, role swapping gives staff the opportunity
to see other parts of the business in action. They act as fresh
eyes on other departments and can ask questions such as
'Why do you do it that way?' to challenge cultural norms
that otherwise would go unquestioned. Not every creative
act has to break ground and transform: equally valid in certain contexts, and certainly of commercial importance, are
the 'incremental ideas' that create a small but important
improvement – just think of any clothes washing product
that claims to be 'new and improved' with added clothes
whitener or an enhanced fragrance. These are incremental
ideas.

Organizational think

There is a danger in all organizations that you must be
aware of if you are committed to putting ideas first and
encouraging your staff to focus on creativity as a way to
improve performance: organizational think.

Organizational think
This is groupthink, but on a business-wide scale.
Groupthink has been defined as a way in which
a group comes to think as a homogenous mass,
deterring the expression of new thinking and
ideas, or individual responsibility. The collective pressure of
the group puts off anyone from disturbing the status quo

with a new idea or a fresh perspective. Organizational think is a term I use to describe a similar phenomenon across an entire business: the same people tend to come up with ideas, while the rest feel it is 'not their place' to have their say or voice ideas.

The issue with organizational think is that the 'ideas territory' of a business becomes very small: the same people have similar ideas because they are generating them in the same way every time. This often involves one person commandeering the flip chart to make sure all their ideas get written up, while ideas they consider below par mysteriously do not make it to the page. Thus the ideas territory is well trampled, not particularly fertile and contained by the immovable fences of organizational think – and it would take a very brave person indeed to scale the fence and explore new ground elsewhere.

Using the idea generation structure I have outlined previously can be an effective way to eradicate organizational think. In such a session, everyone is equal and has the same opportunity to voice ideas without fear of ridicule, as every idea at this stage is treated as a good idea. There are no single 'ideas people' in these sessions, because everyone is considered an ideas person. And as the group is made up of a diverse range of people from all over the organization, the ideas territory is as expansive as it can be: the only limit will be how far the group wishes to explore. In a broader organizational context, by encouraging ideas from every part of the business and creating an environment that fosters collaboration, you can stop organizational think in its tracks.

The creative environment

Have you ever seen the inside of Google HQ in London? It is worth using the search engine of your choice to have a look at this vibrant, highly creative and engaging working environment designed by the Penson Group. Rooms are completely upholstered with green velvet from floor to ceiling, TV screens flicker from the floorboards where they are embedded, allotments are tended by Google employees in the garden, floral wallpaper lines a boardroom, astroturf replaces carpet. With as many meeting (or 'collaboration') seats as there are desks, what does this environment say about the company? There is no mistaking the creative, risk-taking and exciting culture that the interior promotes. Technology is used to facilitate creativity and make a more inspiring place to work: as our personal technology untethers itself from the electricity sockets, so we can create a more flexible and collaborative work environment that promotes ideas.

Lee Penson, founder of the Penson Group, is convinced of the importance of an inspiring work environment to promote better ways of working: 'I can promise you that the more adventurously you think about humans being comfy and efficient at work in the future, the better. It's a massive step towards making work better for employees while improving the company's bottom line. It's a win-win situation.'

THINK ABOUT IT

Think of your working environment, or look around if you are sitting in it. What does it say about your organization? Does it promote creativity? Are there objects, spaces or images that are there to inspire and provoke new thoughts? Does it fire the imagination? Does it encourage people to come together to discuss ideas and take time to think in new ways?

Think back to the question that was posed in the Incubation section (see page 34) of the book: Where do you have your best ideas? Most commonly, people have great ideas anywhere but their desk – in the shower, at the gym, in the bath. These are all places where the subconscious can really get to work on generating ideas, where the conscious mind is not focused on the challenge and the brain is allowed to wander as it wishes.

But it is not always possible to install a gym in the office, or a row of bath tubs, or to have a company dog that staff can take for a walk (unless you are Google). So how can you recreate that space where the brain is at its creative best?

Let's first consider what it is about someone's desk that makes it such a bad place to have ideas. The computer, with its expectant blinking cursor and the inbox stuffed full of messages that require action, is a sure-fire way to mak the brain focus on 'doing' rather than 'thinking'; deadline rather than exploration. And the same with the phone an a mobile – both are terrible interrupters to any train c thought. The desk is also simply the place where a certai type of work is expected, and so sitting down at the des will inevitably set up a mindset of working, when what i really required for creativity is a mindset of playing.

So what other space can be used for creative thinking Many companies that I have worked with cannot dedicate huge amount of space, or feel they cannot sacrifice the on boardroom, as an ideas space (although if meetings tak place in a boardroom full of creative stimulus, this can hav a profound effect on the quality of the output). But even corner of the office can be transformed, and here are just few ideas as to how this can be done:

- Use furniture and objects that make a contrast to a things 'desk'. Use sofas, comfy chairs or beanbags fc seating – it is all about creating a relaxing space to le the mind wander.

- It can be useful to partition off the area to create defined space for thinking: people can sometimes fee self-conscious if they're sitting pondering out on th main work floor. Partitions can also be covered wit images, words and other Random Sparks.

- Have music in the space, to help transport mind elsewhere.

- Have shelves or boxes stuffed full of Random Sparks – if these items are out on display (even pegged on a rigged-up washing line) then they are easily integrated into an ideas session as Sparks, and make the environment more stimulating. Toys and other items are great to have lying around, so people can play with them while they think.

- Have a shelf of books – not about the business you work in, but other topics to inspire the mind; anything from art to racing cars.

- Adorn the walls with prints and images that are colourful and interesting.

- Throw a colourful rug on the floor – another visual cue that this is not a traditional work space.

- Have a ready supply of surfaces to capture ideas as they arise (a large whiteboard, or even better, a whitewall), and wall space or a washing line where flip chart sheets can be displayed. And lots and lots of pens of different colours. Or use a digital flip chart that automatically captures the written page in a digital format.

- Include some plants or greenery – you might not be able to have a walk in the woods every time you need a good idea, but you can bring a little bit of the woods inside.

The key to your ideas space is renewal. Every couple of months or so, change the space around – this does not have to be drastic. Use some throws to change the colour scheme, replace pictures and images with new ones, and bring new Random Sparks into play.

 Don't just rely on a single ideas space to transform your business environment. Use other communal areas to reinforce the message that ideas are paramount. For example, put a Random Spark on a shelf above the water cooler, and change this every couple of days. Or why not put a shelf of Random Sparks in reception, to really broadcast the creativity message? And what about putting a whiteboard in the kitchen, scribbling up a current challenge and asking people to jot down anything that comes to mind? It is surprising how fertile a mind can be when it is hanging around waiting for the kettle to boil. Don't worry about the odd funny comment; provoking laughter is a great way to get the brain into a creative state.

You might not have the space or budget to transform your entire office space, but there is a lot that can be done with a small budget and lots of enthusiasm.

THINK ABOUT IT Why not hold an idea generation session with staff to tackle the challenge of how to transform your working environment into a creative, inspirational space?

Create a place for ideas

So you have created a space for generating ideas – now it is just as important to create a place for ideas to live. In the average two-to-three-hour idea generation session that may run for a business, between 150 and 300 ideas can be generated and captured. It is important that once the shortlist of ideas has been selected, the huge number of remaining ideas are saved somewhere safe and accessible. Just because an idea was not selected, it does not diminish its potential to be used either at another time or for another challenge. It is a huge waste of brain capital not to save all these ideas available for use whenever required – whenever you have a new challenge to tackle, it is always worth reviewing past efforts for inspiration and a possible solution.

An ideas bank is just such a place. It can be as simple as an Excel spreadsheet, where all the remaining ideas are inputted and categorized. This can then be browsed, searched and added to as required. The bank then itself becomes a huge repository for Random Sparks and should be accessible by everyone in the business. Alternatively, an online ideas bank can be created as part of a company's intranet for ease of access.

IF YOU REMEMBER ONE THING

An ideas session involves time and money – think of all the overheads sitting in your ideas space at any given time. Make the most of this brain capital by capturing every idea that is generated, no matter how unpromising it may look. One person's ridiculous notion is another business's competitive edge.

Create a pipeline of creativity

Giving your staff the opportunity to contribute ideas outside of idea generation sessions is an effective way of demonstrating that your business puts creativity at the centre of what it does. Ideally, the organizational culture should be such that everyone feels able to tell their manager, the MD or the CEO about an idea that they have just had, the moment they have it. Sadly, there are many businesses where this is not encouraged, so that no matter how boldly the website states that this is a creative company, deaf ears to ideas speaks volumes about what is really important.

If you open up a route for ideas to travel quickly and freely between staff and also to the senior team, the benefits will be manifold. First, sending a clear message that every person in the business has the opportunity – or, in fact, the responsibility as part of their job – to come up with new ideas, will empower the staff tremendously. Most people want to know that they can have a positive effect on where they work and what they do, and encouraging ideas from all corners of the business will engender a huge amount of enthusiasm, motivation and loyalty.

Second, your staff know their part of your business better than anyone, and can often spot things that no amount of head-scratching by other people will match.

GKN Aerospace believes fully in getting st. involved in improving and developing wh they do, and runs a suggestions scheme for t purpose. Over 80 per cent of staff contribu and one idea saved the business over £10,0 a year – instead of using masking tape to cover bolt ho when spray painting, someone suggested the use of reu able ear plugs!

And third, if you involve everyone in the conversati you get the most out of your brain capital, and your st. will have more fun and engagement at work as th can make things happen and will feel part of a success future.

There are many ways to add new sources to your ide pipeline. New staff are excellent for this, as they ha not yet been subsumed by the existing office cultu and will be able to spot areas that could be improved transformed.

For a large advertising agency, I created initiative called 20:20 Vision. This was a si ple idea-capturing process for all new recru that came into the business. After a couple months, they would be asked to complete short questionnaire about the business – covering wh

ey felt could be improved, what ideas they had about
e business and so forth. This quickly became an invalu-
le source of new ideas and thought-provoking questions
out the best way to do business, and brought best prac-
e and fresh thoughts into the business from a variety of
her industries and competitors.

ollecting ideas

what is the best way to collect all these ideas? At the
ost basic, you could have old-fashioned suggestion boxes
not very high-tech, but I have seen these work in com-
nies, as they require very little effort. Then there are
ftware programmes available to take the suggestion box
line, with built-in review and ranking tools to streamline
e process. Or perhaps you could simply set up a dedi-
ted email address – such as ideas@joebloggsltd.com
that anyone can use to contact the business owner or
nominated, suitable person when inspiration strikes. Or
en a number to which staff can text the idea. Again, use
ur creativity to come up with different options if none
these are right for your business. A company in the US,
ead of the UK in terms of recognizing the value of staff
eativity, has really put its money where its ideas are. Many
the nuclear energy company Bruce Power's staff do
t sit at a desk, so they installed idea kiosks throughout
e plant so that people could walk up to one and submit
idea.

IF YOU REMEMBER ONE THING Whatever method you choose to capture staff ideas, the key is to make it effortless. There should be no obstacle between someone having an idea and submitting it. Asking people to fill out a form in triplicate and send it through internal mail will not have people rushing to find a pen to take part. Having a tablet computer on the kitchen wall so that people can submit ideas while boiling the kettle will make it feel like second nature.

So once there are hundreds of ideas pouring in, what then? It is absolutely imperative that the ideas are reviewed regularly, and that you are in a position to move forward with the best ones. There is nothing more demotivating for people than contributing ideas only to see nothing happen, and you are wasting both time and money asking your staff to think of them if you then don't use them. So whether it be the senior team, the CEO or an appointed cross-function team, an individual or group must have explicit responsibility for reviewing and actioning appropriate ideas.

Selecting ideas

Several organizations that have idea schemes get the staff to review ideas in an 'X Factor'-style competition. A shortlist of the best ideas each month could be published for staff-wide review, not just to select the strongest, but also to build upon them. If you have issued a business challenge to prompt ideas, then remember to be clear about the success criteria so that the ideas selected will solve the challenge. (Any great ideas that are not used should then be put in your ideas bank.)

Companies with schemes such as these will often incentivize staff to come up with ideas, which is a great way to encourage participation. You may set selection criteria – for example, successful ideas will have to save the company money in some way – which can then be linked to the incentive. Perhaps the staff member receives 1 per cent of any savings. Or for every idea selected, the person responsible will receive a gift voucher. Or for the best idea generated each quarter, the prize could be a day's holiday. Whatever the incentive, it is an important element of asking staff to come up with ideas, as it demonstrates that *their* ideas are a valued part of the business.

Talk about it

It is essential that any ideas scheme is visible to all staff, not only so that they can easily participate, but in order to show that the ideas generated are being considered or acted upon. Getting the staff to review the ideas, or vote on them, can achieve this visibility. Equally, you could produce a quarterly 'brain report' to tell staff just how many ideas have come in and which ones are being implemented. Put it in your internal newsletter. Have an ideas counter in reception. Assign ideas champions to head up the scheme and encourage participation. For every idea contributed,

pledge 1p to charity. Gather task forces to implemer
ideas. Write the best ideas up somewhere everyone ca
see. Have a ticker-tape display of ideas as they are sub
mitted. However you do it, make a noise about it; it w
encourage people to get involved, it will make people fe
that their contribution counts and it will firmly demonstrat
that you take ideas seriously.

 Nirvana CPH, a London-based creative produ
tion house involved with helping brands pu
graphics on any surface and creating innovativ
brand expression, is a creative business whic
works with global, creative clients. It is essenti
that Nirvana themselves demonstrate their innovative cre
dentials – to staff, clients, suppliers and potential client
They have devised Pulse, a dynamic collection of image
and posts pulled from their Instagram and Twitter feec
that shows off their brilliant work, as well as interesting an
inspiring images that they capture while out and about. It
a rich, diverse visual scrapbook that encourages people t
comment and join in the conversation – a perfect manife
tation of a creative culture.

Tell stories about the ideas that you have – weave your cre
ative culture and the innovations you create into your bran
story. Stories are one of the most powerful ways to con
municate something, and there are plenty of stories abou

103

eativity that have become business folklore. The Post-it ote, for example, was invented at 3M by accident when chemist attempted to develop a very strong glue and nded up with one that was extremely low-tack. What are e developments and ideas in your own company that are orth telling stories about? Talking about them will make eople keen to create some more, and will be a constant inforcement of your creative culture. Not only that, but will highlight the benefits – demonstrating to everyone at creativity is not a 'nice to have', but is in fact a business sential.

THINK ABOUT IT

Why not hold an idea generation session to come up with innovative new ways to capture staff ideas?

xtending your pipeline of creativity

nce a staff scheme for capturing great ideas is in place, e next step is to extend your pipeline of creativity beyond e walls of your building. Your customers will have a nique perspective on what you do and how you do it, and an prove an invaluable resource in terms of insight and eas. One of the simplest ways to reach out to them is ith a customer survey – not only will this give you insights nd ideas, it can also engender customer loyalty as there nothing that customers like more than being asked their opinion and to then see changes being made in light of their comments.

Customer survey responses may not be filled with great ideas that are ready to implement, but the insights and comments about how your business, products or services are perceived can provide the platform from which an idea can spring. It might be worth feeding a summary of the survey content into a staff idea generation session. I worked with a local ironing business that runs regular customer surveys, and uses comments and insights from the surveys to create new promotions. Recently, a customer commented that she started using the service when she had her first baby. This led the business owner to think about a new target audience that was so far untapped – new mums – and so she created a successful 'new baby voucher' incentivizing new mums to try the ironing service to see how convenient it was. Many of these new customers are now regulars.

There are many other ways to elicit ideas from customers, from dedicated email addresses to online suggestion boxes, just as you would use with your staff.

 First Direct bank, an innovator in the field of banking from their inception in 1987 with their 'windowless branch' concept (only offering telephone banking, and more recently internet banking) launched the Beta Lab in 2010 with the express intention of giving their customers a chance to offer ideas and feedback on new products and services prior to launch. As well as this, the online platform allows customers to submit ideas on any aspect of the business. This gave their customers a chance to have a say in the business they were using, and provided First Direct with valuable market research and a wealth of ideas from new perspectives. Perhaps unsurprisingly, in 2012, First Direct achieved the highest ever *Which?* customer satisfaction survey score of 93 per cent.

Again, the key here is to make the success of the scheme visible by telling your customers about the ideas that are submitted, and more importantly, about the improvements you make as result of them.

It's not wrong, it's just not right yet

Failure. Just the word can make you sigh and hang your head. You've failed. You are wrong. That idea didn't work so let's forget it completely. Even in our formative years at school, failure is hardly tolerated. A question has a right or wrong answer – everything is very black or white, with no room for the grey in between. But that is exactly where ideas can be found – in that murky grey bit, yet to be right but by no means wrong. Having been measured by success or failure, right or wrong, from the moment we step into education, it can be tricky to change our mindsets to accept that the grey area is a valid place to be. But that is what we need to do to embrace creativity.

James Marshall Reilly, entrepreneur and author of *Shake the World*, interviewed top business leaders and entrepreneurs and observed that the most successful do not internalize failure as the majority of people do. Instead, they largely see it as an experience that is the result of variables outside their control – something that at one point or other is inevitable and from which valuable lessons can be learned.

For businesses who deal in great ideas, failure is not termed as such. James Dyson, engineer and inventor of the dual cyclone vacuum cleaner, famously made over 5,000 prototypes of the bagless vacuum. Each one was not quite right, but rather than deem it a failure and give up, he saw it as being simply one step closer to success.

A business culture that accepts that ideas will be not right first time, every time, is one that is receptive to the development of creative ideas and the success that they can bring. Whether it be a service innovation or a new product, the key to sustaining a creative business is to test and develop, using each iteration as a step in the process of creating a fully formed, robust new idea.

An element of speed is also critical in the creative process and the ability to deal with failure. Speaking at the Wired Conference in 2012, Michael Aston Smith, the founder of Mind Candy (the company that created the online social networking game Moshi Monsters) recounted a key lesson in business ideas. Their highly complex game Perplex City was not catching on. Smith described it commercially as 'a disaster' and noted that 'we failed in a long, slow, painful way', as they were unwilling to accept it was not working. Eventually, with one last roll of the dice, they created the hugely successful online world of Moshi Monsters and Smith became a billionaire – but it almost didn't happen, due to their initial insistence on sticking with an idea that just did not work and that nearly sank the company. He concludes of his experience: 'There is nothing wrong with failing as long as you fail fast.' Speed is of the essence in the process of ideas. Allow failure to stick, allow an idea that is not working to remain so, and creativity will soon falter.

Train your people

It is essential that you invest in the brain capital that sits within your business, and this is particularly true of creative skills. As I have quoted previously, a *Harvard Business Review* study showed that 80 per cent of creative ability is learned – so if you are not training your people to think more creatively, you are relying on just 20 per cent of the creative potential that you could be putting to commercial use.

By training your staff, you will give them the skills to think more creatively when they are solving problems, to think more laterally when they are faced with business challenges and to be more divergent in their thinking when they are generating ideas. With these new skills, you can use any number of creative tools – such as the ones outlined later in he book – to their maximum effectiveness. In addition, the eople who come back into the business after training and an demonstrate their creative skills with day-to-day busiess challenges will encourage others to think in new ways.

It can be hugely beneficial to train a number of staff (peraps called your 'Creativity Champions', or 'Idea Angels') to icilitate the idea generation groups. Facilitating groups is skill that takes time to master, and a small investment in a andful of people to enable them to run effective sessions an ensure you are really making the most of the brain capil in your business. Alternatively, you can bring an external icilitator in for those ideas sessions that really need to eliver transformative thinking – there are facilitators who becialize in running creative sessions and it is worth spendg time talking to one or two before you make a decision n who can help you, as it is important that they will fit with bur business and understand your requirements. A good icilitator will model what a great ideas session should look e and bring the creative best out of everyone in the room.

THINK ABOUT IT How could you introduce creative training into your business? As well as half- or full-day courses, could you be more imaginative about it? How about lunchtime seminars that eliver bite-size training over a sandwich? Look around bur business to find people who are already using their eative muscles – how can you get them to share their approach? Or perhaps find people outside the business who have been successful because of their creative approach – can you get them to come and talk to your people and inspire them to think differently?

Measure it

As with any new initiative or change in business, it becomes an open-ended and often fruitless activity without the proper measurements in place to track and quantify success. Whatever you do to make your business more creative, it is essential that you measure it to understand its true value.

How you measure it depends entirely on what you are doing and the success criteria that you have defined – so create your own measurement metrics and timescale (for example, each quarter), and make sure that managers and teams are fully aware of what is being measured and how. Your measurement metrics could include:

* How many ideas have been generated

* How many new ideas have been implemented or brought to market (make a distinction between absolutely new ideas and those that are incremental improvements)

* Which processes have been improved, replaced or streamlined

- How many product and/or service developments have been made

- How is your brand perceived: is the business seen as creative, as full of innovators?

You could also include creative measurement for employees within their appraisal process – this is one of the key ways you can demonstrate that ideas are the responsibility of everyone in the business. So you could measure what their individual input has been into making the business more creative, measured in an appropriate way – from how many ideas sessions they have attended to their involvement in other creative initiatives.

It is essential to make creativity and the pursuit of ideas part of the business values and mission, and communicate this clearly and regularly to staff. In this way, as with other strategic intents and objectives, these creative 'requirements' feed into the appraisal process as a key way to measure individual, team and departmental performance.

Encouraging questions

It is invaluable within a creative business to develop a curious culture – one that encourages people to ask questions. After a few years in existence, every business develops assumptions and 'norms' about how things are done – from how new products are developed, to the service procedure, to how the staff are paid and rewarded. Regardless of how well the business was structured at the outset, time and habit will set this thinking in stone unless a conscious effort is made to remain flexible and open to change. Questions are a powerful creative tool to ensure that organizational 'norms' are still relevant and commercially viable. Simple questions such as 'Why do we do it like this?' and 'How can we do this better?' can be the lifeblood of a creative business.

THINK ABOUT IT

What would happen if you took every process or function in your business one by one, and asked: How can we do this better?

---

3. The Creative Tool Kit

this chapter you will find a wide range of creative think-
g tools that can be used individually or in groups, either
a scheduled session, or in a more ad hoc, 'at your desk'
ay (although I would recommend moving away from your
sk, even if you only plan to spend five minutes generat-
g ideas). If you are in a group situation, you can prepare
few of these tools in advance to introduce as Random
arks. In essence, all of these tools are Random Sparks
hey force new thoughts, associations or insights to help
u solve your problems, and they will all change the way
e group is thinking and lead to a new territory of ideas.

With people who are practised in the process of gen-
ating ideas, many of the stages that these tools teach
e done instinctively. To increase your own creative ability,
oose a few of these creative thinking tools to practise on
egular basis to give your creative muscles a workout. As
u do this, these new ways of thinking will become second
ture and you will find sitting down to come up with 50
w ideas a much easier prospect than before.

ind mapping

nd mapping is one of the quickest, easiest and most
ndamental tools you can have in your creativity tool kit.
vised by Tony Buzan in the 1960s (although versions of it
ve existed for much longer – even da Vinci had one), it is

a method of drawing and linking information in diagram Buzan claims that a mind map 'unlocks the potential of t brain' as it uses a range of cortical skills, combining word images, numbers, logic, colour and spatial awareness achieve clearer thinking, in order to unlock creativity a improve performance.

In essence, a mind map uses a single thought plac centrally on a page (expressed as words or an image), fro which associated thoughts are placed radially in curv spokes, with each separate branch using a different colo to help stimulate the brain more fully and differentiate t different topics or themes. I use mind mapping regularly a wide range of applications, and use Buzan's basic met odology to map ideas and explore concepts. However have found that sometimes it is not practical to have different coloured pens with me, and so over the years using this technique, my mind maps are certainly no mo than a 'version of' a traditional Buzan mind map.

Using the one I made when I first sat down to plan t book as an example, this is how I create a mind map:

1. Get a piece of paper, the bigger the better. Or if po sible, get a flip chart or a whiteboard. The paper shou ideally be used in landscape orientation.

2. In the centre of the paper or board, write the thought challenge you wish to explore. Draw something as w if you can – using images stimulates the mind. Do

worry if you are not an accomplished artist – just so long as *you* know what it is, that's all that matters. I scribbled a picture of a book with a light bulb on the cover.

3. Now branch off the centre with a line, and write the first associated thought or theme that comes to mind. This might be a logical thought – the concept of 'introduction' came first to me – or something random or seemingly 'out of order'. This is the beauty of mind mapping – there is no such thing as out of order, as you are working around a central theme, not making a list.

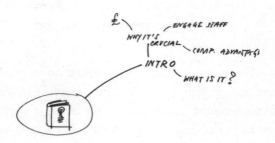

4. Next I jotted down a number of ideas that came to me that I thought could be part of the introduction. One thought – 'why it's crucial' – then inspired further exploration, which I noted down as smaller spokes from the idea that spawned them.

5. Once you have exhausted that line of thinking, with as many smaller spoke patterns as needed, go back to the

centre and let another idea or thought come to you, and start the process over again.

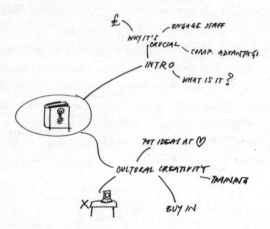

You will see above that I have moved on to my second spoke, using doodles where I can. I have also added in another thought to the Intro spoke of the diagram, as it came to me while thinking about cultural creativity but fitted better in the introduction. Being able to edit and add easily as you go along is why mind mapping is so flexible as a thinking tool, and why I rarely use lists any more – even my to-do list is a mind map.

5. Continue to add thoughts and spokes, until your map starts to resemble the branches and twigs of a tree, or until you run out of space on your paper; in which case get some more paper, stick it to the edges of your first piece and carry on.

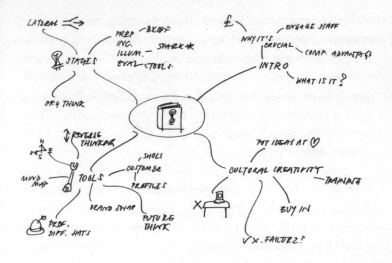

So this is my mind map after about five minutes or so – a first 'brain dump' or exploration of possible book content. At this point, I broke off and went and made myself a cup of tea, another essential tool in any creative person's tool box. This is not as facetious as it might sound – when you have seemingly exhausted your mapping, take a quick break. When you return you will see more connections and have further ideas you can add in.

Because of the layout of a mind map, it engages the visual side of the brain, which makes reviewing information and ideas that much easier. You will find that you can easily spot priorities, themes and great ideas within a mind map.

Mind mapping is also a great exercise to do in a group, either as a stand-alone creative thinking exercise to solve a challenge or as a Random Spark exercise, as words and thoughts that come to you as part of the mapping process will act as Sparks that help you think laterally and give you new ideas. You can pick up on a word or phrase and get the group to explicitly use this as a Random Spark. It is useful for the person who is drawing the mind map to use different colours for each spoke, to really engage the group and make different themes stand out.

Sometimes the thoughts and ideas people come up with while mind mapping will seem far removed from the central challenge, but this is a normal part of idea generation. For example, with a central challenge of how to get the staff to collaborate more closely to encourage creativity, someone might randomly say 'canteen' (they were thinking about where the best collaboration currently happens), prompting someone else to say 'cheese sandwich' and then another person to say 'salt and vinegar crisps'. This all sounds like a creative cul-de-sac, but it is these sorts of contributions that can provide the Random Spark to inspire a fresh idea. The 'crisps' image might provoke someone into thinking of those crisps with the small packet of salt in that you shake into the bag – which could lead to an idea that each person's name is put in a virtual 'sachet' online, and creative task forces are selected by 'shaking' the random sachets into a project 'bag'. Or that collaboration should happen over a nice lunch. Or that the best collaboration project is rewarded with a slap-up dinner, with a cheese sandwich as the consolation prize.

When you are mind mapping and find you have no more spokes or thoughts you can add to a branch of thinking, do not labour too long trying to come up with new ideas. Simply move back to the centre and start another branch – this will help you maintain momentum and encourage new thoughts to come to you. You can add ideas back into previous spokes as they occur to you.

Icebreakers

Whenever you are generating ideas in a group, an ice-breaker is a great way to get everyone focused and to change their mindset. As we have explored previously, at the office people are naturally in 'work mode' and therefore are in a 'doing' frame of mind. An icebreaker helps change their mental agenda to one of exploring and playing.

Icebreakers are not meant to be too taxing. Instead, use an icebreaker that gets the group to recall something, rather than invent it – in this way, people will feel confident from the outset that they can contribute, which helps them relax and will encourage further contributions.

It is important that the facilitator asks everyone in the group to contribute to the icebreaker. Giving people a 'get out from answering gives the whole group implicit permission not to contribute, and those that do not get any air time during the icebreaker will feel more reluctant to speak up once the session gets going.

As previously mentioned, the icebreaker does not have be related to the challenge – and if it is not, lead to some great Random Spark material – but it can be if you feel this s appropriate.

Some examples of icebreakers are:

- **Reveal**: Tell us something about yourself that no one in the room knows about you.

- **Journey**: What is the best journey you have ever taken and why?

- **Stuck in a lift**: Who would you like to be stuck in a lift with?

- **Achievement**: What is your greatest achievement?

- **Lessons**: What was your favourite lesson at school and why?

- **Cartoon character**: Who is your favourite cartoon character and why?

Doodle you: Get each person to draw a quick self-portrait without anyone seeing. Collect them up and get the group to guess who's who.

- **Desert island**: You are stranded on a desert island. Apart from the essentials to ensure your survival, you can take three things. What would they be?

- **One word mind map**: Put a word in the middle of a blank mind map on a flip chart that is related to your challenge – e.g. if the challenge is about how to create creative ideas spaces in the building, you could chose 'creative' or 'idea'. Go round the group asking them to contribute a thought, word or idea to populate the mind map.

- **Have you ever**: Get each person to jot down something that they have done (e.g. bungee jumping) that they think no one else in the group has. Then each person reads their card out, with a show of hands for others that have also done it. The winner is the person that elicits no raised hands.

- **Dice questions**: Write up six numbered questions on the flip chart, such as: What is your favourite book? What are you most proud of? What's the best advice you've ever received? What is your musical guilty pleasure? What would your dream job be? If you could have one drink with any celebrity, who would it be? Each person throws a dice and answers the corresponding question.

- **Extra time**: If you were given two extra hours today, how would you spend them?

It is worthwhile capturing the icebreakers on paper so that you have a great collection of Random Sparks that you can introduce to the idea generation session as you go.

Random Sparks

I have talked previously about how essential Random Sparks are to the creative thinking process and what sorts of Sparks you can gather to help you think laterally and with different perspectives. Random Sparks can be anything and everything (and all the tools listed in this section are in effect Sparks themselves), but as a quick summary, examples of Random Sparks are:

- Toys

- Magazines: You can rip out images or headlines to spark new thinking

- Books: You can ask people to pick a word from a specific page

- Drawings

- Words: Print out random words on a sheet of paper, hand out to the group

- Objects: Strange items with no obvious purpose can really get the ideas flowing.

Whatever you use as Sparks to create new thinking, ask the group some prompt questions to help get the ideas flowing, such as:

- Think about a key property of this Spark. How could you apply this to the challenge?

- How does this Spark help solve my challenge?

- What is the idea that comes to mind when you look at your Spark?

Silent Post-its

This is a great creative thinking tool to use at the beginning of a group session after the icebreaker, but it can be equally effective at any point in the idea generation process. As there is no speaking allowed, it provides a very different group dynamic, which will change thinking within the group – and it is a great way of getting ideas from those in the group who are more reticent about speaking up.

1. Give everyone a pad of Post-its.

2. Ask everyone to write three ideas down to solve the challenge, each on its own Post-it.

3. Go round and ask each person to read out his or her ideas before sticking them on the wall.

4. Then ask the group what other ideas come to mind now that they have heard the others' Post-it ideas.

There is another version of Silent Post-its that works well for generating ideas on your own:

1. Write each idea you have on a Post-it and stick them all up on a wall or flip chart as you go.

2. Once you have exhausted your train of thought, pick one of your Post-its and stick it on another blank space on the wall.

3. Now consider this idea, and write further ideas that are inspired by it around it, like a mini mind map.

4. Once you feel you have no other ideas to contribute, pick another Post-it from your original pool of ideas and start again.

 Writing ideas on Post-its can be a useful way to capture them – not only can you move them around to provide further inspiration, as above, but you can also start to sort, prioritize and theme them very easily.

Flip the Thinking

A sure-fire way to stop creativity dead is assumption. However, when solving any challenge, it is natural to make assumptions. If we are asked to consider how to improve the daily commute, we might well assume that the solution has to involve travelling to work. But if we remove that assumption, we can then explore home working as a viable solution. Or if we are thinking of ways to make bath time more enjoyable for kids, there may well be an assumption that bath time has to involve a bath. But if it doesn't, then we can consider washing them in the paddling pool – much more fun (though not advisable in the winter).

So, this 'Flip the Thinking' tool will help you break down the assumptions inherent within your challenge to provide fresh perspectives and insight:

1. State your challenge using the 'How to ...' challenge format.
   E.g. How to tell everyone about our new product.

2. Identify an element of the challenge headline that could be an assumption.
   E.g. That you need to tell everyone.

3. Flip this thought.
   E.g. You tell no one.

4. The flipped thought is not likely to be a practical idea, so now consider your flipped statement and see how this can become an idea.

   E.g. You create a limited edition product that only a few lucky people can receive.

   Or You 'leak' the launch on social media to garner interest.

   Or You tell no one where to get the product; instead you release online clues and get lots of PR from this.

5. Once you have exhausted your flipped statement, find another assumption and flip it.

E.g. Assumption: You tell people. Flip: You show people.

Ideas:

Give free samples for trial in exchange for feedback and endorsement.

Make viral videos of people using the product.

Create a 'try it out' road show to let people experience the product.

USEFUL TIP If you run out of assumptions to flip, try restating the 'How to …' challenge headline in a new way – this may well uncover new assumptions about the problem. So if you had a challenge headline of 'How to make bath time more enjoyable for kids' but had exhausted the ways to flip the assumptions, you could restate it as 'How to get the kids clean while entertaining them'. This then uncovers the assumption that it is you who has to entertain them – what if you used other means of keeping them occupied, like listening to a story on a waterproof iPod speaker? Another way to flip assumptions if you are in a group is to take the first six ideas, which are inevitably going to be the most obvious ones, and flip the assumptions or ideas in them.

What are the assumptions latent in your business as a whole? Consider each department, function or process in turn and jot down a list of assumptions. The more radical your thinking, the more assumptions you will spot. Now look at your list of assumptions. It is a worthwhile exercise to analyse each one to see if it is still relevant. Choose an assumption to flip – what new ideas come up that could transform, or at the very least improve, your business?

Brand Swap

New ideas are often born from considering a field unrelated to the matter at hand, and 'borrowing' the concepts found therein. Nature has long been plundered to such effect – take the much-cited example of George de Mestral, who went for a walk in 1948, got covered in burrs and used these little seed pods to inspire the invention of Velcro. But there are plenty of other fields that can be used to create new insights. One that I use to great effect in idea generation sessions is brands, as they evoke certain reactions and thought processes in people that can then be combined with the challenge to be solved.

1. Print out a range of famous brands – say between eight and twelve – on separate sheets of paper or as a grid. It is important that you use the logo, not just the name of the company. The visual clue of the logo will provoke

a much clearer response than words alone. Pick brands that have a strong identity, such as Virgin, Apple, Nike, Innocent drinks, Smart cars etc. Ideally, choose brands that are famous enough that everyone in the group will recognize them and understand what they stand for, as well as brands that provoke an emotional response in people. For example, you could use Mini, which is considered a fun and adventurous brand.

2. Hand out the brands to the group, or pick one to consider yourself.

3. Ask: 'How would this brand solve the challenge in question?'

4. Capture the ideas that come to mind until you have no more to add, and then you can either get the group to swap brands, or pick another yourself.

The ideas generated in Brand Swap will not necessarily be 'ready to use', as they were inspired by a brand that could be very different from yours. But it is a valuable exercise to consider the challenge in terms of how others would interpret it.

For example, say your challenge is to create amazing customer service in store. You pick Innocent drinks as your brand swap and ask yourself how they would solve this problem. They might:

• refresh their customers with 'pick me up' smoothies

- create a grassed area with deck chairs to help shoppers relax

- take products in a branded van to the customer's door

- have fresh fruit at the counter for customers to nibble on while they queue.

You might think the grassed area an idea worth developing – but grass and the outdoors might not be suitable for your brand. This idea could then be easily adapted to create a chill-out area in store for promotions or events.

 Other brands will not necessarily have the same values and approach as you, so do not expect every idea to be a good fit with your desired outcome. However, it is a great tool to help switch perspectives, break out of any organizational think and get some 'fresh eyes' on your challenge.

Standing in your Customers' Shoes

It is always imperative to ask: 'Who are you solving this challenge for?' It is all too easy to tackle a business challenge without really taking time to consider the target audience. If the challenge is an internal business problem, then the 'customer' of that challenge is the staff. However, it is often the case that challenges have customers outside the business, who may well have a very different profile to that of the people who are coming up with the ideas to solve the challenge.

How effective would a 53-year-old male be at coming up with appropriate solutions for a challenge aimed at a sixteen-year-old girl? I would posit that he may well lack a natural understanding of the target customer. Ideally, a business would undertake in-depth customer profiling to really get under the skin of the lives, desires, purchasing habits and so forth of their customers, but sometimes this information is hard to come by. Customer focus groups can be a great way to gain an understanding of the target audience, but they can be time-consuming and costly.

So another way to better comprehend your customer is to undertake the Standing in your Customers' Shoes exercise:

1. Using customer data that you already have, create ten customer profiles. The aim here is to really bring each person to life. Give each customer a name, state their age, their job, where they live, their family status, their hobbies and so on – whatever is relevant to the challenge you are solving. For example, if you are a sportswear business, your customer profiles should contain information about the sports they undertake, perhaps how often they do each sport, and their sporting ambition. The information that you put on each customer profile will not necessarily be true – this depends on how much actual customer data you have – but it will be your best

guess. It is useful to print them out on cards, so that they are easy to hand out and then store for future use.

Robert, 35
Lives in Kent with his wife
Project manager
Loves golf, squash and
watching Arsenal
Wants to run the marathon

2. To really get under the skin of these customers, ask each person in the idea generation group to take a card and spend some time considering this person, thinking about what is important to him. Then you can ask the group to come up with ideas to solve the challenge (for example, how to encourage customers to make us the destination retailer for all their sporting kit) as if they were that customer – so using the sample card above, someone might answer 'I wish I had Arsenal-branded golf wear' and they would be answering as if they are Robert – thus bringing a new perspective, one that is closer to the target market, to the ideas.

CASE STUDY

I facilitated a three-day idea generation session for a fuel retailer who wanted new ideas for their European-wide summer promotion to run in all of their petrol stations. Around the table sat twelve European managers, all in suits, all over 30. But the promotion was aimed at families driving through Europe on their summer holidays, and my biggest task was to get these directors to stop seeing the challenge through their own eyes, as this was leading to a lot of organizational think. So I handed out customer profile cards to each of them with a variety of holidaymakers on them, both adults and children. It was at the point at which the German marketing director announced that he was six years old and needed to go to the toilet, and asked for an ice cream, that it was obvious that standing in his customer's shoes had transformed his thinking and fundamentally changed his perspective.

3. Once you have elicited ideas from everyone in the group, they can swap the customer profiles with each other and carry on generating ideas.

Idea Building

It is useful to have an exercise within the idea generation session that gets people doing something other than just sitting and talking, particularly if the session is a long one.

I have sometimes asked people to get up and swap seats with someone else as a way of getting the blood circulating and literally giving them a new perspective.

Idea Building is an exercise in this vein, as it gets people writing and using their hands. It's a little bit like that game where a group writes a story together: one person writes a line, and then passes it on to the next person who writes the next line, and so on.

1. Hand out a piece of A4 paper to each person in the group.

2. At the top of the page, each person should write an idea for solving the challenge.

3. Ask everyone to pass the piece of paper to their left.

4. On receiving their neighbour's paper, each person should read the idea written down there and build on it, writing a new, improved or revised idea beneath it before passing it on again.

5. Continue to write down ideas and pass them on until each piece of paper is back at its original person. Everyone then quickly reviews all the ideas in front of them and then reads out in turn what they think is the strongest idea on the page.

6. Collect all the sheets and keep them, as they are full of potentially great ideas!

If you really want to get the group up and moving, you could use flip chart sheets stuck to the wall instead of sheets of A4 paper. Arm everyone in the group with a marker pen and use the same process. This will really energize the group, so it is a good Spark to introduce if the group is running out of ideas – and particularly good if there is a post-lunch lull.

Job Jump

Finding a new perspective from which to consider a business challenge is half the creative battle. With Job Jump, it is different professions that provide new insights.

1. Consider one of the Job Jump jobs below in relation to your challenge. You can make Job Jump cards with a job written on each one, so that you can easily have several rounds of Job Jump within a group session.

2. Generate ideas relating to your challenge from the point of view of a person doing this job. You can think about the sort of person who would have this profession, the activities they undertake, what they wear, where they do it, the attributes of someone doing this job – all these thoughts and more will provoke new ideas.

3. Once you have exhausted the ideas from one profession, pick another.

Sample Job Jump list

- Spaceman
- Artist
- Musician
- Racing car driver
- Shopkeeper
- Drug dealer
- Dog walker
- Window cleaner
- Fireman
- Builder
- Street sweeper
- Talk show host
- Doctor
- Cowboy
- Spy
- Paramedic
- Taxi driver
- Farmer
- Baker
- Pirate

This list represents just the first twenty professions that I came up with – create your own list and keep refreshing them as you use them.

TRY IT NOW!

Imagine your challenge was to get more people into your shop (or choose a challenge relevant to your business). Pick Pirate for your first Job Jump, and consider how a pirate would solve the challenge. You can also consider the behaviours, appearance, attitude or any other attribute of a pirate to help inspire your ideas. Give yourself a few minutes and see how many pirate-inspired ideas you can create – write them in the space below.

How to get more people into my shop

How did you do? When I tried this for a couple of minutes, I came up with:

- Having a treasure chest in store that customers can use as a lucky dip to win products

- Printing a map reference on each receipt, which refers to a treasure map in store. Whoever's reference hits a square on the map where treasure is buried wins a prize

- Giving every visitor to the store the chance to win a cruise

- Giving customers half a coin on a postcard – they have to come into the store to try to find the other half

- Giving one loyalty coin for each purchase in store to redeem against 'treasure'

- Running a store competition where staff have to come up with ways to attract people into the store, and the most successful employee will win the 'treasure' (i.e. days off, vouchers etc.)

Once you have run out of inspiration with your current Job Jump, pick another and start coming up with ideas again.

Fairy Godmother

Sometimes it is difficult to think big and bold, forgetting the obvious obstacles that stand between your challenge and a solution. Often when generating ideas in a group, these obstacles and perceived difficulties are not aired, thus creating a subconscious block to progress. Acknowledging any obstacles can be a useful way to either remove or circumnavigate them. Using a Fairy Godmother always helps, I find.

Say to the group (or yourself): 'Your fairy godmother will grant you one wish to help you solve this problem. What will it be?'

Many of the responses to this question will illuminate the current blocks in thinking, such as: 'I wish we had a million pounds to solve this' (obstacle: the budget is too small), 'I wish Lady Gaga would tweet about us' (obstacle: we haven't got enough 'voice' or buzz about us) or 'I wish I could reward great customer service on the spot' (obstacle: managers have no autonomy to reward staff).

Then ask what the solution could be if the wish was granted – these ideas will be different from those that came before, as you have theoretically removed the obstacle that was confining the creative thought process.

You can ask the group any number of Fairy Godmother questions ('Your Fairy Godmother will grant you one more wish …'), as there are often numerous obstacles that can get in the way of really bold, new ideas. The ideas may not be practical, but these wild, ridiculous notions often contain the seed of something great that can be made to work. For example, if the Fairy Godmother granted the wish to have a million pounds to make everyone in the business more creative, the idea might be to employ world-renowned artists, film makers, writers and musicians to talk to the staff about being creative. In reality, this will never happen. But the thought could inspire the business to give staff trips to the gallery, or to a concert, or to start a reading club or a creative writing group – all things that could really put creativity and inspiration at the heart of a business.

 It is natural for the brain to throw up obstacles in the path of solving a challenge, and left to its own devices, it will make an assumption that these obstacles are immovable. With this creative thinking tool, however, you can force the brain to remove the obstacle, freeing up a whole new route to innovative and original ideas.

The 9-Spot Grid

This tool takes a number of elements of the challenge at hand and uses them as Random Sparks, forcing new connections between otherwise unrelated concepts.

1. Create a 9-spot grid on an A3 piece of paper, or on a flip chart or whiteboard if you are generating ideas in a group, like this:

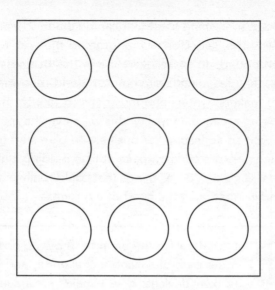

2. Identify three different elements of your challenge. For example, say the challenge is 'How to reward staff for delighting customers and going the extra mile'. Three elements of this challenge could be: staff, customers and extra mile. In the first row of your 9-spot grid, you are going to write these three facets of your first challenge element, one in each spot.

3. Consider your first element and allow two thoughts to come to mind about it. So in this case, my two facets of 'staff' are: caring and fun. Write these in the two spots directly below 'staff'.

4. Do the same with the next two elements of your challenge, taking 'customers' and 'extra mile' in turn. My grid now looks like this, with facets of 'customers' in the second column and facets of 'extra mile' in the third:

5. Now randomly select two spots and draw a line between them. Consider these two words and come up with an idea related to how they combine. For example, I might pick 'fun' and 'money'. Reminding myself that the challenge is 'How to reward staff for delighting customers and going the extra mile', my first idea might be for managers to give out play money to staff for every

great customer service act. Staff can save the 'money' and trade it for days off. My second idea could be that great customer service should be rewarded with charity pounds, which are donated to a staff member's charity of choice each month.

6.   When you exhaust the ideas from combining two spots, pick another two and repeat. If you are feeling brave, try picking a spot from each column and create an idea using three spots as your inspiration.

 Do not spend too much time completing the 9-spot grid. It doesn't matter which elements of your challenge you select. If you allow your brain to combine the spot words freely, ideas will always come.

Doodle It

Using your hands while you are generating ideas is a great way to free the subconscious part of your brain to do what it does best.

1.   Make sure everyone in the group has a paper and pen.

2.   Ask people to draw their version of the challenge that you are trying to solve. Emphasize that drawing skill is not required, and in some ways the more abstract the

art the better. So, the challenge 'How to improve my daily commute' might inspire a drawing of someone in a car, or someone reading a paper, or a sketch of an angry face with smoke coming out of the ears, or just a page of scribbled symbols representing expletives – anything goes.

3. You can then show the group everyone's drawings (it will usually provoke some good-humoured laughter at the range of interpretations on display) and then either leave them all pinned up for the rest of the session, or ask people to pick one and let that drawing help to inspire an idea.

USEFUL TIP Doodling is a great way to aid thinking, particularly when you are trying to come up with creative ideas. Carry a pad and pen with you, so that if you are on the bus, waiting for a train or waiting for a meeting, you can doodle away to your heart's content. Never stare at a blank page when you are trying to be creative; simply put pen to paper and see where it goes.

Scamper

Scamper is a well-used creative thinking technique devised by Bob Eberle, author of books on the subject of creativity. It uses the principle of juxtaposing previously unrelated notions to create new thinking and insights. This is often referred to as 'forced association'.

 Forced association is attributed to Alex Osborn (1888–1966), who also developed brainstorming. It is a technique whereby a number of random words are forcibly linked together and related to the topic at hand. The psychological theory behind this is that holding two dissonant thoughts or words in our heads jolts the subconscious brain into giving you what you need – i.e. a good idea – to remove the discomfort of this jarring partnership.

'Scamper' is an acronym that you can apply in relation to your challenge headline. If you are working in a group, read out these prompt questions. As ever, take note of every idea that comes up, no matter how weird or impractical. The acronym breaks down as shown opposite.

So, for example, with a challenge of 'How to create an amazing shopping experience for customers online and in store', we could Scamper the problem like this:

- **Substitute** 'amazing' with a Random Spark of 'drum' and have a live band in store and original music playing online

- **Combine** 'online and in store' and have a store-cam

ACTION	PROMPT QUESTIONS
Substitute	What can you substitute in your challenge? What can you use instead? Other people? Other places? Other approaches? Other Random Sparks?
Combine	What can you combine to solve this challenge? Combine businesses? Combine the people involved? Materials? Purpose? Create a group?
Adapt	What can you adapt for a solution? What ideas can you 'borrow' from other fields? From nature?
Modify	Change the way you look at the challenge. Change its meaning. Change the words. Change its shape.
Put to other uses	Can you find other purposes for or relationships with your challenge? How could an outcome have further benefits beyond the obvious?
Eliminate	What can you remove? What is not necessary? Can you streamline? Can you eliminate obstacles?
Rearrange	What can be rearranged? People? The environment? The process? The words in your challenge?

online so shoppers can have a sense of the retail environment and the buzz of the crowds

- **Adapt** 'shopping experience' to 'day out' and offer customers the chance to win a luxury shopping day with a chauffeur, lunch and champagne

- **Modify** the assumption that people want to do their own shopping and offer a personal shopper for the day instead

- **Put to other use** the enjoyment that customers will get from shopping by creating customer vox pops that show other potential shoppers how great the experience is

- **Eliminate** all the stores and build a walk-through environment online instead with avatar shop assistants and virtual trying-on

- **Rearrange** the words 'shopping experience' and 'customer' so the challenge is instead to create an amazing customer. You could hand-pick your favourite customers for VIP shopping evenings.

I have thought up only a single idea for each action, but it is valuable to spend time creating as many as you can for each one. Alternatively, if you have less time you could just pick one of the Scamper actions at random and use that to create new thinking.

Object-ivity

A great tool to have up your creative thinking sleeve, Object-ivity takes a random object and uses it to create new thinking through forced association – using actual objects or images of the object rather than words – to stimulate, engage and bring the object to life.

1. Present the group with a random object, or image of the object – or give each person a different object.

2. Ask them to consider it for a moment, then come up with an idea to solve the challenge based on it.

3. When ideas run out, pick another object and start again, or ask the group to swap their object with someone else's.

 Get a cardboard box and create a selection of Object-ivity objects. Don't limit yourself to actual objects that fit in the box – if you want a mountain, put in a photo of one. Keep topping up or replacing objects so that these Random Sparks remain fresh. You can always ask the participants of your next idea generation session to bring a random object with them to use in the Object-ivity exercise.

Items to use for Object-ivity could be:

- a torch
- a plane
- a screwdriver
- a mirror
- a hairbrush
- a cork
- a zip
- a sofa
- a pair of scissors
- a fairy
- a test tube
- a bed
- a cat
- a cloud
- fire
- an egg
- a postcard
- a field
- a lorry
- a magician

Ask a Stupid Question

This tool is a great way to break down assumptions about the challenge you need to solve, as well as making sure there is not an obvious but brilliant solution right under your noses. Stupid questions can provoke laughter, which, as previously discussed, is the perfect state in which to be creative.

1. Consider your challenge. For example: How to develop a new range of health drinks.

2. Ask a stupid question, such as, 'Why can't someone else come up with the new range?' While on the surface this might seem to be the response of someone who simply can't be bothered, within that stupid question are a number of ideas, such as: get the customers to invent the flavours instead with instore Invention Days; get an Olympic athlete to put their name to the range; get a health-conscious chef to devise the flavours; do sampling in gyms and get healthy people to try the drinks and select their favourites to be produced.

There is no end to the stupid questions that you can ask about a challenge, and each one will lead you to a new way of thinking. So, for this challenge, other stupid questions might be: Why does it have to be a drink? Why is there a range? Can we use an existing drink? Why does it have to be healthy? And so on.

Celebrity Wisdom

The phrase 'celebrity wisdom' may sound like something of an oxymoron, but this tool is a great way to liven up an idea generation session, often provoking laughter and always giving brains a new perspective from which to consider the challenge.

1. In advance, choose a number of celebrities to use, either by writing their names on pieces of card, or by printing out a photo of each. So, you might choose:

- The Queen
- Lady Gaga
- Delia Smith
- Tom Jones
- Charlie Chaplin
- David Beckham
- Gordon Ramsay
- J.K. Rowling

and so on.

2. Get each person in the group to pick a celebrity.

3. Ask: 'How would this celebrity solve the challenge?'

4. You can then get the group to swap celebrities and come up with other ideas.

For example, your challenge might be: How to get all internal departments to share ideas and knowledge more freely. Lady Gaga might provoke ideas about holding 'show and tells', or pinning every idea onto an ideas mannequin in reception. Gordon Ramsay might lead you to think about representatives from each department holding a regular masterclass to demonstrate their knowledge, or having knowledge sharing/ideas sessions at a local restaurant, or chopping the departments up once a quarter and getting a slice of each department working in another part of the business for the day.

 If you are preparing a 'pack' of celebrities, make sure they are all well known enough that people will not be stumped by them. The more obvious the celebrity's personality, talent or behaviour, the better. And don't be limited by contemporary celebrities – feel free to include the dead and the fictitious.

Stakeholder Compass

Very often a challenge will involve a number of different 'stakeholders' – people who have a connection to and/ or a stake in the challenge and its ultimate solution. So, if your challenge is 'How to create a fun, inspiring High Street festival to celebrate the town', then your stakeholders will be visitors, residents, shop owners and the police, as all these groups will be affected by or involved in the activity in some way. You can also have a set of stakeholders that are predominantly internal within your business – a challenge to work on tenders more effectively would have several different departments or specific individuals as stakeholders. It is important that all stakeholders of a challenge are considered, and this tool is an excellent way of ensuring all of their perspectives are taken into account.

For example, to create your High Street festival challenge stakeholder compass:

1. Map the key stakeholders onto four compass points:

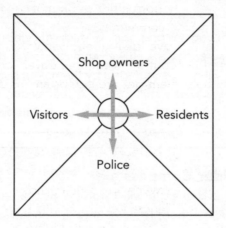

2. Now consider each stakeholder in turn and ask: how would they solve this challenge? Write all the ideas in the stakeholder's quadrant before moving on to the next point of the compass.

For example, shop owners might want the festival to be advertised over a 50-mile radius, to have stalls outside each shop to highlight their wares, for parking restrictions to be lifted or to be allowed extended opening hours.

Residents might come up with ideas such as celebrity visits, a way to celebrate the community, a place to leave the children while they enjoy the festival, text alerts for when activities are about to start or a local talent competition.

The police might have ideas about local buses being free for festival-goers, a group of volunteers to be festival peacekeepers, or opportunities to promote policing as an essential part of the community.

Visitors might have ideas about wanting local and historic information about the town, free travel, an interactive map app to help them get around, or an 'insider's guide' to the town.

 There can be more than four stakeholders in any challenge, so you can create further compass points between the four to include them. You can split the idea generation group into pairs or smaller groups, and ask each smaller group to look at just one or two of the stakeholders.

Perfection

It can sometimes seem impossible to reach a solution from a starting point that seems so far away from success. Perfection is a tool that flips the creative process on its head, by focusing on the ultimate, perfect solution and assuming it has already happened. This helps prevent the 'that wouldn't work' syndrome that can hamper ideas before they have a chance to be developed, and untethers ideas from practical thinking that insists on knowing *how* it will be done as well as *what* will be done. This is how to do it:

1. Remind the group of the challenge headline.

2. All together or in smaller groups, build a vivid picture of perfection in the future. Write (or draw) what you consider to be the ultimate solution to your challenge in a specified time frame – you may wish to put this solution six months, twelve months or ten years in the future, whatever is most relevant to the challenge. Spend some time delving into detail to really make the picture of the perfect solution and outcome come to life.

3. Think about the people who at this future point have experienced this perfect solution – be they customers, people within your business or others. Write down quotes from them after they have experienced this amazing solution.

4. Now step back from your perfect solution. You can now reposition yourselves back in the here and now and ask questions that will uncover a route to this solution, such as:
   • What did we do to get here?
   • How did this happen?
   • What three things did we do to create this?

- What didn't we do?
- Who helped us?
- What was our first step toward perfection?

You can imagine a number of perfection scenarios to envisage several possible outcomes to your challenge.

Random Images

As with a lot of the tools in this section of the book, Random Images creates a range of Random Sparks to inspire new lines of thinking and fresh ideas.

Random Images can be used in an idea generation group, but it is particularly good when coming up with ideas on your own, particularly if you are on a train, waiting for a bus or away from work. You can either create a 'pack' of random images on cards, or use your smartphone – running an image search for 'random images' will produce pages of just that. Click on one, consider it and let it inspire you.

Ideas Pool

This technique is a great way to change the pace and dynamics of the session by getting everyone in the group to work individually.

1. Give each person a pad of Post-it notes.

2. Introduce a Random Spark and ask each of them to use it and write down their ideas for solving the challenge

on the Post-its, placing each Post-it in front of them as they go, creating a pool of ideas from the group.

3. After each person has put down two or three Post-its, ask them to pick up a Post-it from the person to their left.

4. The idea written on their neighbour's Post-it should inspire new thoughts, and these should also be written down, one per Post-it, and placed in front of the person.

5. Then ask everyone in the group to take a Post-it idea from the person to their right and let that inspire new thinking.

6. After more ideas have been added to the ideas pool, gather up all the Post-its and read each idea to the group, before sticking them up on the wall and moving on to more idea generation.

Question Time

Questions are a powerful way of provoking different thought processes – ask someone a question and the brain will automatically try to find an answer to it. Questions are the key to creativity, and they inspire the brain to come up with new thoughts – the important thing to remember with questions that inspire ideas is that there is no one right answer.

1. Consider your challenge headline.

2. Each person in the group writes down a question they have about the challenge.

3. In turn, the questions are read out.

4. Now, going round the room, the group should each contribute an idea as to how to solve the challenge. These ideas will not necessarily address one of the questions, or seemingly bear much relation at all to the questions that were read out, but fear not – that is not the point. The questions will provoke the brains in the room to think about the challenge in a new way, which in turn leads to an idea.

For example, your challenge might be: 'How to drive more potential customers to our website to learn about our products.' The questions that the group ask might be: 'Why can't we pay them?' 'Why can't the website go to them?' 'Why can't we show them the products?'

Which in turn may then prompt ideas such as:

- Loyalty points for every website visit

- Discounts for referring a friend from the website

- Limited-time product discounts that are online-only

- Online demos of products

- Screens in shops to show the full product range and information

- Product information and discount emails to potential customers

- Employees to video themselves using the products to demonstrate to potential customers.

 You can choose to be more focused about how you use the group's questions. After they have each written down a question, pick one (such as 'Why can't we pay them?'), and turn it into a fact: 'We will pay them to go to the website.' Now you can ask the group to come up with ideas to expand upon and explore this statement. Once you have harvested the ideas from this question, you can pick another and do the same.

---

4. Evaluating Your Ideas

Creativity is about the ability or talent to create. It's about generating ideas. Innovation is the implementation of the new. Innovation means taking creative ideas and making them real.

Paul Sloane, *Lateral Thinking Skills*

So, you have run an idea generation session, or generated a long list of thoughts on your own, and now have hundreds of new ideas. Now what? This chapter shows you some effective, simple tools that will help you evaluate your ideas and make sure they stand the best chance of succeeding – it's all about turning creativity into innovation.

The process of evaluation is about understanding the value of the ideas that you have generated, and developing them enough to be able to analyse their worth and impact. Implementing ideas is the best way to reinforce your commitment to creativity. Doing nothing with your ideas, or failing to evaluate them prior to bringing them to life, can not only be highly demotivating for staff, but can also do serious harm to your bottom line.

In terms of time and resources, this stage is as important as generating the thoughts themselves – after all, does it really do justice to six people who sat in a room for a day working hard to generate great ideas to have one person quickly read through the output with a red pen and somewhat arbitrarily pick the idea that will be put into practice?

It is sensible to ensure that the ideas are reviewed by

a small group of people – people with the appropriate expertise to have an understanding of what it would take to turn them into reality, but equally importantly, people who have enough 'corporate bravery' to select new or radical ideas.

Corporate Bravery (and its nemesis, **Corporate Fear**)

Corporate Bravery is essential for a creative business. It is shown by people who are not afraid to challenge the status quo, who would never utter 'Well, that's just the way we do things here' and who will gladly take calculated risks in order to push the business forward. Businesses with Corporate Bravery will embrace new ideas, be constantly evolving and often lead their field. Businesses run by those who have a lot of Corporate Fear are those that will wake up one day wondering when their competitors got so much better than them.

The evaluation techniques are divided into two sections: first-stage tools and second-stage tools. First-stage tools are those that you will need when you are dealing with a large ideas pool – if you have any more than about twenty ideas. From a typical idea generation session there may well be over 200 ideas, so these tools will give you a way of quickly highlighting a small shortlist of ideas that can then be analysed in more detail, using tools outlined for the second stage.

With all the evaluation tools described here, it is important to spend time choosing the tools that are most appropriate for the challenge at hand. It may also be relevant to run your ideas through a number of the tools, looking out for recurring themes as you do.

First-Stage Evaluation

There are four first-stage evaluation tools outlined here. It is up to you how to apply them to your ideas – often, just using one of the tools will suffice. Remember, first-stage evaluation is all about getting the strongest ideas out of the large ideas pool so that you have a manageable number of ideas to take through to the more detailed second-stage evaluation.

The evaluation snapshot

I recommend that this evaluation tool is run at the end of every idea generation session, and have outlined the details in chapter 1 (see page 69). But in summary, the snapshot works as follows:

1. Ask the group to review all the ideas generated.

2. Each person should write down the two or three ideas that they feel best answer the challenge headline. Vary the number depending on the size of the group, as you don't want a shortlist of 50 ideas – ideally, you are looking for about fifteen.

3. It is imperative – as with every evaluation tool – that the emphasis is not just on picking a great idea, but a great idea that *solves the problem*. There will often be strong ideas created within the ideas session that do not do this and it is important that these are not erroneously selected. (This is why an ideas bank is so important, so these great ideas can be stored and used another time.)

4. Each person reads out their selected ideas and they are written up on the flip chart as the shortlist.

5. You should see a consensus start to occur within the shortlist – either with specific ideas or specific themes. This is a good indication of where the final idea may lie. For example, answering a brief about how to wow customers and win loyalty, there might be a few ideas around the theme of making the customer feel like a VIP, another couple about incentivizing purchases in a variety of ways and some more about a customer event of some sort. It is useful to look out for themes, as they can provide useful focal points when you start the evaluation process.

You can also give the group stickers to place next to the ideas they think best fit the brief, which is a quicker method but does run the risk of groupthink – where an idea that attracts a few stickers will start to attract a lot more as people want to be seen to be part of the group consensus.

The evaluation snapshot does not mean that the hundreds of ideas that do not make the shortlist will not be considered. It is important to review the entire list with the key stakeholders (some of whom may not have been part of the idea generation session but are now part of the evaluation). The snapshot can be run again with the evaluation group – and those ideas that appear on both the original shortlist from the ideas session and the new evaluation group should definitely be considered further.

Idea Clusters

Sometimes it is difficult to analyse the different themes that came up within the idea generation session. Idea Clusters let you see the variety of approaches within which different ideas sit. This is useful in order to see where lots of ideas are clustered around one theme (suggesting that this would be a rich area for further exploration), but it can also show where other approaches have been ignored. So if you have run a session about encouraging repeat purchase and create Idea Clusters from the output, you may see that there was nothing about offering money off the next purchase. It is worthwhile to consider whether this is because there were much stronger themes and ideas, or if, in fact, it would be valuable to add this as a new Idea Cluster at this point.

1. Go through all the ideas generated and group them

into themes. For example, ideas for the challenge 'How to encourage people to visit a physical store' might be themed around in-store events, email communication, competitions and so forth. Decide on the most relevant themes for your challenge. Write each theme and the ideas related to it on a separate flip chart sheet.

2. Once you have defined all your Idea Clusters (usually with a final 'miscellaneous' cluster to accommodate those few ideas that do not naturally fit within any other cluster), ask the evaluation group to take each cluster in turn, review the ideas within it and select the strongest idea that best answers the brief. If they like, the group can spend time 'creating' the strongest idea in each cluster by combining elements of more than one idea so that no great elements of any one are lost.

3. The strongest idea from each cluster forms your short-list and enables you to start second-stage evaluation.

Traffic Lights

Traffic Lights is another great first-stage evaluation tool that will quickly let you review each idea in turn. It is best done in pairs – two people can challenge each other's pre-conceptions about ideas so that no undue influence can be exerted, while steering clear of the danger of a larger group, where too much discussion and disagreement will grind the process to a halt.

1. Arm yourself with a batch of round stickers in three colours – red, orange and green. Alternatively you could use three marker pens or different-coloured small Post-its.

2. Reread the challenge headline and the brief. It is helpful to have the challenge headline printed out on a piece of paper and pinned up in your eyeline.

3. Start to review the list of ideas that have been generated. For each idea, mark it with one of the three traffic light stickers:

   Red: This idea will not progress further as it does not solve the problem.
   Orange: This idea may have potential but needs further thought.
   Green: This idea will make the shortlist.

   The essence of this process is speed, with minimal discussion. If there is disagreement between the pair, err on the side of generosity – so if one wants it to be red and the other orange, it is awarded orange.

4. Now you have an orange shortlist of ideas that need further work and a green list that will be evaluated in more detail. The red list can be filtered straight into your ideas bank.

If the evaluation group is larger, then Traffic Lights can be run simultaneously in pairs, whereby orange and green lists are compared at the end of the process and ideas that are frequently marked green are all put through to further evaluation.

Stakeholder Questions

This tool is adapted from the evaluation criteria used by the supermarket Tesco to identify strong ideas within their business. Stakeholder Questions is a great way of evaluating an idea from the different perspectives of everyone who will be involved with the potential solution.

1. Identify the main stakeholders in your challenge. For example, if your challenge was 'How to put creativity at the heart of our business' you might have staff, management, business and clients or a combination thereof as the stakeholders.

2. For each stakeholder, decide upon the one criterion that is essential for them when solving this challenge. So, for staff in this example, it might be that they want the chance to be more creative, while for the business it might be to improve its reputation, and for the clients it might be to receive a more innovative and improved service.

3. Once you have written down the stakeholders and their criteria, run through each of the ideas and ask:

- Will it make the staff more creative?

- Will it improve the business's reputation?

- Will it give the clients a more innovative and improved service?

4. If an idea provokes a 'yes' for each of the stakeholder questions, it goes through to the final shortlist. If an idea fails on one of the stakeholder questions, it is put in a 'holding list' requiring further work.

Second-Stage Evaluation

Once you have whittled your ideas pool down to a manageable number – anything from three to twenty – then you can carry out the second-stage evaluation. This is a more in-depth process, looking at different facets of the potential solution and quantifying its strengths and weaknesses in relation to the other ideas under consideration. You can just run your shortlist of ideas through one of these evaluation tools, or choose more than one. It is always beneficial to evaluate using at least two of these tools, as they all focus your critical thinking about the ideas in slightly different ways.

Prior to further evaluation, you may find that the shortlist of ideas needs some development. For example, for a challenge as to how to make your business more creative you could have the idea 'Run a monthly creative competition' on the shortlist. But this idea could mean lots of different things to different people, and a consensus as to what that idea entails needs to be reached before further evaluation.

So the first thing to do for each of your shortlisted ideas is to take an A4 sheet or flip chart sheet and, in a small group, flesh out the idea in more detail. Consider:

- **How the idea might work in reality**: Using the example above, you might decide to run a quarterly staff creativity competition, using a different creative medium each time (photography, writing, painting, cooking …).

- **Who it involves**: This particular competition could be for all staff, with a team of Creativity Champions who promote and judge the entries.

- **Any further points to note**: All the work could be showcased in reception or online; the competition could be opened up to clients.

- **Any questions**: In this case, what is the budget for prizes? How do we judge?

It is not imperative that you find out answers to all these questions, but the more you can, the more accurate your subsequent evaluation will be.

This process is not by any means designed to flesh out every detail or practicality of the idea – this should happen *after* second-stage evaluation – but it is a very useful process to undertake to give you enough information to make an informed judgement. The process is also a great way to uncover new facets of the idea – for example, there may have been some doubt about the commercial benefit of running a creative competition for staff, but once the idea was developed and notions of promoting the work online or including clients came to light, it was shown to have more benefits than first thought.

Criteria Scoreboard

This evaluation tool is a great way to start considering all the relevant factors that will influence final success. It is quick and simple to set up and provides an excellent way to judge your shortlist of ideas side by side.

1. Select between five and eight critical criteria on which to judge your ideas. These might be cost, timings, innovation, business reputation, and so on.

2. Create your Scoreboard by drawing a table with the criteria in a column on the left-hand side, and the titles of the ideas under consideration in a row across the top, like this:

	Competition	Staff Away Day	Creative Masterclasses
Cost			
Time to implement			
Raise creative bar			
PR-able			
Resource required			
Unique to us			

4. Now consider each idea in turn, and give each one a score of between one and five against the criteria. So for the Cost criterion, a maximum score of 5 means it will come in under budget, while a score of 1 is for ideas that may well blow the budget. Do not be tempted to give 'halves', as this just complicates things unnecessarily.

If you wish, you can weight the most important criteria so that the strongest ideas that best answer the challenge will be highlighted appropriately. So, each criterion in the Criteria Scoreboard above currently has a maximum scoring of 5. However, if the key driver of the project is to raise the creative bar within the business, then you may wish to give that criterion a maximum score of 10, so ideas that fulfil that part of the brief will get more points. It is useful to create a column next to the criteria list to show any weightings, so a completed chart might look like this:

	Top Score	Competition	Staff Away Day	Creative Masterclasses
Cost	5	5	3	1
Time to implement	5	3	2	2
Raise creative bar	10	8	6	9
PR-able	5	1	0	5
Resource required	5	2	3	4
Unique to us	5	4	1	5
TOTAL	**35**	**23**	**15**	**26**

So, in this Criteria Scoreboard, the creative masterclass idea is the frontrunner, with the staff competition just behind. At this point, it would be well worth spending more time developing these ideas fully, while discarding the staff away day idea (by putting it back into your ideas bank for another day).

THINK ABOUT IT

The criteria selected for the Criteria Scoreboard can obviously have a huge effect on whether an idea is put forward for further consideration, so it is important that time is spent choosing the right criteria against which to judge the ideas. It is a valuable exercise to canvass opinion from all the key stakeholders as to their measures of success – you may feel that raising the creative bar is the most important outcome, but if the person holding the rubber stamp of approval believes that the idea's PR potential is the most crucial factor, then that should be reflected (and possibly weighted accordingly) in the Scoreboard.

SWOT analysis

The SWOT analysis came out of a research team at Stanford Research Institute in the 1960s. It is an evaluation tool that looks at four key factors of a business, situation or idea.

The model assesses the following:

Strengths: The positive attributes of the idea

Weaknesses: The factors within your control that could detract from the success of the idea

Opportunities: The potential, both now and in the future, of the idea

Threats: The factors that could threaten the success of the idea.

1. Grab a flip chart and write your ideas in the middle of a page – you will need one page per idea.

2. Divide the page into quarters, labelling each with a SWOT heading.

3. Take your first shortlisted idea and take each SWOT quarter in turn, noting down your responses to the following prompt questions:

   Strengths:
   What benefits does this idea bring?
   What is unique about this idea?
   What are its key strengths?

   Weaknesses:
   What is likely to cause problems with this idea?
   What are the key weaknesses of this idea?

   Opportunities:
   What future opportunities might this idea bring?
   How could it be developed in the future?

   Threats:
   What elements of this idea are out of your control?
   What are the key threats that could stop it being a success?

   So, for the idea of creating an app for mobile devices to show your product range:

STRENGTHS	WEAKNESSES
– cuts cost of physical catalogue	– no in-house know-how to create app
– easy to update	– untried format for us
– no competitors have one	– crowded 'app market place'
– shows us as tech savvy	– long development/testing period needed?
– encourages younger target market	– will need marketing support
– reflects online presence	– alienate older customers?
– can drive people online to shop	

PRODUCT APP

OPPORTUNITIES	THREATS
– will present us as tech literate	– competitors may beat us to market with app
– can extend for in-app purchases	– initial app to be simple, but may be easily copied
– can create dialogue with customers via app	– may not create stand-out in app market so underused
– create games to showcase product lines	– simple to use could mean boring to use?
– range of apps	

4. Once you have carried out a SWOT analysis on your shortlist, you are then in a position to review all your ideas to see which are faring well.

5. There is a further step you can carry out with your SWOT analysis, which is critical if you are going to develop any of the ideas further. Review each quarter in turn, considering the following:

   Strengths: How can we exploit these strengths to their full potential to maximize success?

   Weaknesses: How can we address the weaknesses to eradicate or minimize them?

   Opportunities: How can we exploit these opportunities to their fullest?

   Threats: How can we prevent these threats from becoming a reality?

Stakeholder Compass

This evaluation tool builds on the Stakeholder Compass format from the Creative Tool Kit section, using the different positions and perspectives of key stakeholders to evaluate an idea.

1. On a flip chart sheet, draw your compass, which should represent all the important stakeholders involved in the problem. So, if you have a shortlist of ideas to potentially solve the problem of how to create a great buzz around the launch of your new book, the Stakeholder Compass would look like this:

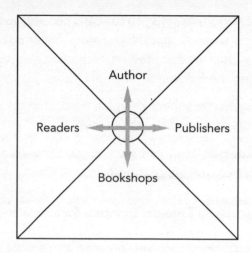

If your challenge involves more than four stakeholders, then create up to another four points of the compass to include them.

2. Before you start the evaluation process, it is important to consider the ideal outcome that each stakeholder would prefer. On a Post-it, write the best or most important outcome for your first stakeholder, and stick it in the relevant stakeholder segment. For example, the author's outcome might be 'critical acclaim', while the publisher's might be 'huge sales'. It is useful to figure out these ideal outcomes, as each stakeholder will measure the success of an idea differently.

3. Take your first shortlisted idea and go round each

point of the compass, noting down the positives and negatives of the idea from the perspective of each stakeholder.

4. Once the compass is complete, tally up the positives and negatives in each stakeholder segment, and then an overall positive and negative score. This gives you a rough indication of how the idea will score against others that you are evaluating.

5. Repeat the Stakeholder Compass for all your shortlisted ideas.

6. Once all your ideas have been through the compass, you can compare their scores. This will help you gain clarity on your shortlist. You can consider:

   • Whether one idea has significantly more positives than others

   • Whether one is racking up a lot of negative points

   • Whether there is one stakeholder that is consistently being failed by the ideas

   • Whether any of the ideas score evenly across all the stakeholders

   • Which ideas produce positive points that most closely match the stakeholders' ideal outcomes.

After running all your ideas through the Stakeholder Compass and considering the results, you should have a good idea where the strongest ideas lie on your shortlist.

The Jury

When there is a group of you evaluating ideas, The Jury can be a great way to start the process. It is quick, fun and asks people to make rapid decisions. This can be a useful way to begin to evaluate the strengths and weaknesses of ideas without getting bogged down in discussion – further development can come later once the jury has decided which ideas have enough value in them to pursue. Ideally, the jury will consist of people who were not involved in the original idea generation process, so they will come to the challenge with fresh eyes and have no vested interest in any of the ideas. A jury of between three and six people will work fine.

1. Create a paragraph of description about each idea under consideration, mindful that you will be pitching each idea to the jury and each pitch should be two minutes or under. Aim to be as clear as you can about how the idea might work, who it involves and what the likely outcomes could be. Returning to the earlier idea about creating an app for mobile devices to showcase your products, the pitch could be something like this:

   We have a great, diverse range of products, appealing to a wide customer base. The product app is a perfect way to showcase these products in an ultimately portable, easily updatable and user-friendly way. It will feature all of our products, arranged in categories, with a search function to allow customers to easily look up items by price or item. We can easily add new products as we get them and with great photography and the possibility of creating short video clips of products in use, make them look irresistible. Initially, it will make a great companion to our catalogue, but with paper prices and print costs increasing year-on-year, it will render the catalogue obsolete in three years, saving approximately £300,000. The product app has huge potential for development, including games to showcase our products in more detail and in-app purchase potential, as well as functions that really enhance the customer experience, such as an instant review tool and links to social media sites that could raise our brand profile within critical new target markets. We can see that the initial investment required to create the product app would be repaid within eighteen months and the brand benefits could be huge. It is the future of how we present our products to the customer.

2. Give each juror a piece of paper or card for every idea you will pitch to them, along with a marker pen and a copy of the challenge headline.

3. Pitch your first idea to the jury, then ask them to write a score out of ten on one of the pieces of paper, bearing in mind that the idea must answer the challenge headline.

4. If you wish to collect further information from the jury, you can then ask them to turn the paper over and write what they think is the strongest element of the idea that they have just heard, and which part of the idea, if any, is the weakest. Finally, they should jot down a question that they have about this idea.

5. Collect the papers, staple them together and mark with the idea to which they refer. Now repeat this exercise with all the ideas you have shortlisted.

6. You can now add up the scores to see which idea the jury felt worked the best. If you have asked the jury for extra information, review this too. It is valuable to get an insight into where people think the strength of an idea lies, as well as what they consider to be the downsides. Their questions may uncover areas of your solution that will need clarification, and all this can be a great way to help develop the idea.

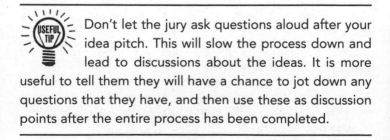

Don't let the jury ask questions aloud after your idea pitch. This will slow the process down and lead to discussions about the ideas. It is more useful to tell them they will have a chance to jot down any questions that they have, and then use these as discussion points after the entire process has been completed.

Do the Maths

It is useful to compare your shortlist of ideas from a financial perspective as part of the evaluation process.

1. Create a grid that includes all the financial measurements you wish to use. These criteria could include cost of development, materials costs, cost of time of those involved, costs to trial or prototype, or any other relevant factors you can think of. Ideally, you will be aiming for accurate figures and this may take some time, but failing that, use internal expertise to make your best estimates, with a proviso that the evaluation results are unconfirmed at this stage. You can then also include projections of what the idea will generate in terms of profit. Select the financial criteria that you feel best represent the ideas. So your Do the Maths grid could look like this:

	Department costs	Materials	Resource	Prototype/ trials	Manufacture	Income/profit 0–6 months	Income/profit 7–12 months
IDEA 1	£	£	£	£	£	£ /£	£ /£
IDEA 2	£	£	£	£	£	£ /£	£ /£
IDEA 3	£	£	£	£	£	£ /£	£ /£

2. Then score each idea against the criteria, putting in values against each one.

3. You can then add up the costs and potential profits of each idea and compare them against each other. It can provide interesting points for discussion – for example, if one idea has high development costs, it might be worthwhile to spend time looking at alternative ways to do this.

Weigh it up

This quick evaluation tool is a visual way to consider the pros and cons of an idea.

1. Take a sheet of flip chart paper and stick it on the wall in landscape. You will need one sheet for each idea.

2. Draw a horizontal line across the page, with a central 'pivot' point, as if you were drawing a simple pair of scales, like this:

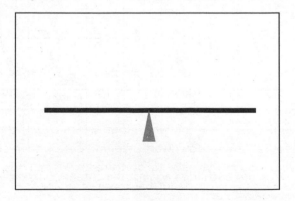

3. Now take a pad of Post-its, and consider your first idea. What are the pros of using this idea? What are the positive elements of this idea? Write each pro on a Post-it and stick it on the left-hand side of your idea scales.

4. Now consider all the cons of running with this idea. What doesn't work about this idea? What are the problems? Write each con on a Post-it and stick it along the right-hand side of your idea scales.

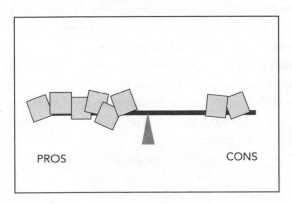

PROS   CONS

5. Once you have weighed up the pros and cons of all your shortlisted ideas, you can get a clear picture of which are the strongest. Imagine that each pro and con weighs the same: on which idea scales would the pro side be tipping downwards (i.e. more pros than cons)? What would you have to do to remove the cons, thus pushing the pro side further toward the floor?

In summary, these six evaluation tools can help to clarify which idea you should be pursuing. It is worth repeating that you can run your ideas through several of these tools to help you decide which ideas are the strongest and which you should pursue, as each of them will shed new insights and raise questions that are essential in helping you develop the strongest idea possible.

Implementation

So, you have run your idea generation sessions, evaluated your shortlist and selected the most viable idea. Now it is time to put your plan into action.

I use a couple of implementation tools with clients at this point to kick-start this process. At this stage, it is all about planning and understanding any potential obstacles or pitfalls that could derail the implementation process and affect the idea's success.

These implementation tools are a great way to bring together a project team or task force, particularly if the group is made up of people across the organization who do not usually work together.

Crossing the River

This implementation tool is all about getting from one river bank (the here and now) across the river to the other side (the finished implementation of your idea). It is useful to map the river crossing on as large a sheet of paper as possible. I have a roll of white paper that I run from one end of a boardroom table to the other, or use to cover the entire length of a wall. This is particularly useful with a group of people, as everyone can see what is happening and contribute accordingly. Working on such a large scale also means it is much easier to go back and add in stages as they occur to you.

1. Draw a river bank at the left side of the paper, and mark it 'Now'. Draw the other bank right at the other end of the paper, marking it 'Completion'. Connect the two banks with a wavy line, representing the river.

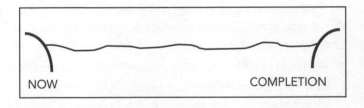

2. The idea of Crossing the River is to build a succession of 'stepping stones' across the water, joining up 'Now' with 'Completion'. Each stone represents an action or task that the project team must undertake to implement the idea.

3. Get a pile of stepping stones – either Post-its or sheets of paper, depending upon the scale on which you are working.

4. Start to write down each action required to move the idea from 'Now' to 'Completion'. As you write an action on a piece of paper, lay it or stick it on the river as one of your stepping stones, positioned roughly where that action will take place in relation to the river banks – the start and finish.

5. When you think you have put all your stepping stones in place, go back and review the river crossing step-by-step, trying to spot any actions or tasks that you have forgotten.

6. Once complete, the stepping stones will have created a detailed project plan that can then be analysed further.

7. Review the stepping stones in turn again, this time marking each one with the names of the people who will be responsible for that task. There should be no stone left unnamed. Doing this ensures not only that everyone in the team has to take responsibility for elements of the implementation, but it is also a good way to check that everyone has a similar number of tasks to execute.

8. Then, as a group, you can identify the sharks. Sharks are obstacles or issues that could pop up along the way and prevent you crossing the river to completion. Look at each stepping stone again. Think critically about what could go wrong and what obstacles could prevent

you from reaching the next stepping stone. Wherever a shark occurs, draw its fin (a black triangle) and note down in a few words what the shark is (e.g. 'trial fails' or 'stores refuse to stock'). So your river might look something like this:

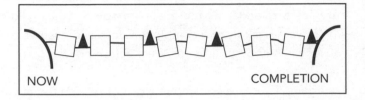

NOW   COMPLETION

Now you can address each shark in turn, exploring ways to prevent the obstacle from occurring, or devising a contingency plan should it happen. The best method of avoidance or prevention can be written on a Post-it and stuck under the relevant fin, along with the name of the person who would be responsible for getting rid of the shark. This way, you have an undercurrent of action plans that will become active should any of the sharks appear as implementation progresses.

With the Crossing the River implementation process, the more time you spend at this stage, the easier and more predictable the actual implementation is likely to be. Time spent analysing likely sharks that could throw the project off course will mean

187

that even if you cannot prevent the shark from appearing, you have a plan in place to deal with it.

___

Implementation Timeline

An alternative planning tool to Crossing the River is the Implementation Timeline. It works on a similar principle, but uses a calendar as the 'planning spine', which allows you to work back from a completion date and ensures that you factor in enough time for every action point required.

1. Again, if you are working in a group to plan the implementation, it is useful to create a large-scale timeline on which to work. Use the full length of a boardroom table, or stick flip chart sheets end to end to cover a wall.

2. Draw a line the length of the paper: this is your timeline. Decide upon your timescale for implementation – for example, you may wish the idea to have been fully implemented within three months. Whatever timescale you choose, the final date should be written at the far end of the timeline, with today's date at the nearest end.

3. Now divide your timeline into smaller segments of time. So with a three-month implementation time, you may wish to divide the line into weeks, or with a year-long implementation target you might want to do it month by month. At each new segment, write in the date, week or month number. Whichever time blocks you

use, it is imperative to mark them with the date or unit number, as this will help to keep the project on track as it progresses.

4. Away from the timeline, get a stack of Post-its and jot down all the action points and tasks that the project demands. Once you have exhausted this, start to place each Post-it at a relevant point along the timeline. Having laid out all the action Post-its, review them as a group and add in any tasks that were forgotten.

 If you have an action that takes a fixed period of time to achieve – such as carrying out market research – create two Post-its for this: a start and stop action. In this way, you can see when this activity starts on the timeline, but you have also committed to a time or date by which this will be completed. Leaving open-ended tasks on your timeline that simply have a start date runs the risk of them not being completed, which will then have a knock-on effect on all the tasks that come after it.

---

5. Once this is complete, review the timeline in its entirety. It is important to be realistic about how long tasks will take, and to make sure there are no 'hot spots' on your timeline where there are a large number of tasks – even though it might theoretically be possible to achieve them all, it pays to be practical about how much will

actually get done. If needed, re-space the Post-its so that the activities are not crammed so tightly together.

6. Finally, allocate people or teams to each task so that everyone knows exactly what part they have in implementing the idea and when they need to complete their activities.

The process of evaluation is essential in creating and sustaining a successful creative business. But there needs to be an element of bravery, where evaluation stops and the idea starts to live. However, it is always beneficial to test your idea, and you don't want to fall into the trap of waiting too long to do this – as discussed earlier, if you're going to fail, it's better to fail fast. Take inspiration from software companies, who do not wait for perfection before they release new software. Instead, they get it as close to perfect as they can, but release it knowing it still has room for improvement. These beta versions, often released to a small number of customers who will give valued feedback in return for being among the first to use the software, will then be adapted and improved until the product is ready to be fully released. And if the idea doesn't deliver on your success criteria? Make sure you have a process in place to capture everything you've learnt from it, and then do something different – and better.

Summary

So, with tools to help you evaluate your ideas and a way to plan out those crucial steps to help make the idea a reality, this exploration of how to be more creative ends. We have looked at why it is so important for individuals and businesses to spend time honing their creative muscles. The four stages of creativity – preparation, incubation, illumination and evaluation – give a simple structure to understanding what is involved in coming up with an idea, and with practice, these stages will happen naturally and seamlessly within an individual's brain or a business's culture, given the right time, space and encouragement. Oh, and more practice.

If you are involved in business, the section on how to grow a culture of creativity will have hopefully given you a myriad of ways to foster the creative intent required to put ideas into the lifeblood of an organization and get creativity pumping into every area. It does not take a fortune to make a business more creative; simply a little bit of time, energy and commitment.

At the heart of the book lies the creative tool kit, which you can dip into whenever you need a creative spark to help you solve a challenge. As I have discussed, these tools are flexible enough to be used by one person with a pencil and the back of an envelope, or applied to a more formal group session. Take time to try out all of the tools and be open-minded – I guarantee that even those that you feel are of little relevance to your challenge will provoke interesting and new responses.

And the final section provides a number of tools for evaluating all those ideas that you will be coming up with to ensure that you think critically and logically about the strength and potential success of each idea.

Whether you intend to use this book to make you a more creative person, to help solve a specific challenge or to transform your business into one where ideas are at its heart, I hope the tools and techniques in it will make a real difference.

In an age where both product and process can ultimately be streamlined by technology and outsourcing, where consumers can shop all over the globe to get the cheapest product and where a truly original product or service has an ever-shortening window of uniqueness before a gaggle of cheaper, faster, better 'me too!' products or services spring up, there is increasingly only one differentiator: creativity. It really is becoming even more a case of 'innovate or die'.

Business leaders must make it their priority to create a culture where ideas are encouraged and celebrated. The business vision and the creative charter will define the attitude of a new breed of creative companies, where everyone is measured in part by the ideas that they bring into the business, where striving for better and constant evolution of business practices is commonplace and where there is a continual pipeline of ideas to bring to life.

I truly believe that for a business to survive and thrive in the coming years, it must take creativity to its heart and empower its people to do the same. And there is no less urgency for individuals to embrace a more creative path, applying fresh ideas to how they go about their life, shape their career and their interests. It is not necessarily the safe path, trodden by businesses and people who went before. You will be plotting a new course, sometimes in uncharted territory, and occasionally on rocky ground. There may be a map, but you may have to throw away that map and draw a new one before you have finished. But it is the only path to take if you are serious about creating a sustainable competitive advantage. Take a sturdy pair of boots, a pair of open eyes and your brain. It will be a trip worth making.

And if you are ever in need of a quick creative pick-me-up, then head on over to www.creativeconsulting.co.uk/spark, where I have created my own online Random Spark generator. So whether you are in a cab, walking the dog or boiling the kettle, a Random Spark to get your creative juices flowing is only a couple of clicks away.

Do you have thoughts, comments or great creative tools that you use and would like to share? I would love to hear from you: jodie@creativeconsulting.co.uk.

Further Reading

A Whole New Mind: Why Right-Brainers Will Rule the Future by Daniel Pink (2008, Marshall Cavendish)

Disciplined Dreaming: A Proven System to Drive Breakthrough Creativity by Josh Linkner (2011, Jossey Bass)

Out of Our Minds: Learning to be Creative by Ken Robinson (2001 and 2011, Capstone)

The Leader's Guide to Lateral Thinking Skills: Unlocking the Creativity and Innovation in You and Your Team by Paul Sloane (2003, Kogan Page)

The Art of Innovation by Tom Kelley (2002, Profile)

What Would Google Do? by Jeff Jarvis (2011, HarperCollins)

The following are great online resources for general creativity and business:

www.fastcompany.com
A magazine dedicated to reporting about how the 'fast companies', entrepreneurs and those at the cutting edge are doing what they do.

www.99u.com
Insights on making ideas happen.

Also of interest is a BBC Horizon programme, *The Creative Brain: How Insight Works* which was aired on BBC2 on 14 March 2013. It is available to view at www.youtube.com/watch?v=C2L0t-EN2Yo at the time of publication.

Index

Notes

You can use the following pages to make your own notes on any of the exercises in the book.

Notes

Notes

Notes

Other titles in
the Practical Guides series

A Practical Guide to NLP

ISBN: 9781785783906
eISBN: 9781848313255

A Practical Guide to NLP for Work

ISBN: 9781785783265
eISBN: 9781848313811

A Practical Guide to CBT

ISBN: 9781785783845
eISBN: 9781848313231

**A Practical Guide to
Mindfulness**

ISBN: 9781785783838
eISBN: 9781848313750

**A Practical Guide to
Emotional Intelligence**

ISBN: 9781785783234
eISBN: 9781848314382

**A Practical Guide to
Child Psychology**

ISBN: 9781785783227
eISBN: 9781848313293

A Practical Guide to Management

ISBN: 9781785783784
eISBN: 9781848314252

A Practical Guide to the Psychology of Success

ISBN: 9781785783890
eISBN: 9781848313316

A Practical Guide to Building Self-Esteem

ISBN: 9781785783913
eISBN: 9781848313668

*A Practical Guide to
the Psychology of
Relationships*

ISBN: 9781785783289
eISBN: 9781848313606

*A Practical Guide to
Positive Psychology*

ISBN: 9781785783852
eISBN: 9781848313736

*A Practical Guide to
Ethics for Everyday Life*

ISBN: 9781785783302
eISBN: 9781848313712

A Practical Guide to Happiness

ISBN: 9781785783241
eISBN: 9781848313637

A Practical Guide to Philosophy for Everyday Life

ISBN: 9781785783258
eISBN: 9781848313576

A Practical Guide to Sport Psychology

ISBN: 9781785783272
eISBN: 9781848313279

A Practical Guide to Body Language

ISBN: 9781785783883
eISBN: 9781848314375

A Practical Guide to Assertiveness

ISBN: 9781785783319
eISBN: 9781848315228

A Practical Guide to Getting the Job You Want

ISBN: 9781785784651
eISBN: 9781848315242

**A Practical Guide to
CBT for Work**

ISBN: 9781785783333
eISBN: 9781848314351

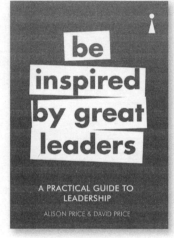

**A Practical Guide to
Leadership**

ISBN: 9781785783296
eISBN: 9781848315280

**A Practical Guide to
Family Psychology**

ISBN: 9781785784729
eISBN: 9781848315365

**A Practical Guide to
Entrepreneurship**

ISBN: 9781785783814
eISBN: 9781848316270

**A Practical Guide to
Treating Eating Disorders**

ISBN: 9781785784668
eISBN: 9781848317451

**A Practical Guide to
Overcoming Phobias**

ISBN: 9781785784675
eISBN: 9781848316904

A Practical Guide to EFT

ISBN: 9781785784682
eISBN: 9781848316966

A Practical Guide to Personal Finance

ISBN: 9781785784705
eISBN: 9781848317475

A Practical Guide to Persuasion

ISBN: 9781785784712
eISBN: 9781848317468